The Antifragile Christian

How Faith Grows Through Struggle

Sidney Anderson, PhD

AR Consultancy LLC

An AR Consultancy LLC Book

The Antifragile Christian: How Faith Grows Through Struggle

Cover design by Md Waheduzzaman Manik

ISBN 978-1-971262-06-2 (paperback) | ISBN 978-1-971262-07-9 (ebook) | LCCN 2025927250

This book offers educational content and perspectives on Christianity and religion based on research, observation, and conceptual frameworks. The author and publisher provide this material for informational purposes only. Nothing in this publication constitutes psychological therapy, mental health treatment, clinical counseling, or professional psychiatric guidance. The author and publisher have endeavored to ensure quality and accuracy in this work. However, no guarantees are made regarding the completeness, reliability, or applicability of the content. Readers must evaluate whether the concepts and approaches discussed are appropriate for their individual circumstances. No warranty of suitability for any specific purpose is expressed or implied. Should you experience significant emotional difficulties, mental health challenges, or psychological distress, seek guidance from a licensed mental health professional. The frameworks and strategies in this book are educational tools, not clinical interventions. This publication does not replace professional mental health evaluation or treatment.

For author inquiries: standersonbooks@gmail.com

Contents

Introduction V

1. Beyond Resilience 1
2. The Historical Pattern 10
3. The Spiritual Gymnasium 23
4. Small Failures, Big Learning 36
5. Skin in the Game 51
6. Raising Antifragile Children 68
7. Engaging the Culture 85
8. The Long View 102

Introduction

A Faith That Couldn't Survive

The text arrived at 2:47 AM. "Mom, I can't do this anymore. Everything you taught me was a lie." Anna stared at her phone in the dark bedroom, heart pounding. Her daughter Gail had been pulling away for months, ever since her best friend died in a car accident three days before their high school graduation. Gail stopped praying. Then she stopped going to church. Then she stopped pretending she believed any of it. "Where was God?" Gail had screamed at Anna the night of the funeral. "I prayed for Lily every single day. Every day, Mom. And he let a drunk driver kill her two miles from home." Anna had offered the answers she knew: God's ways are higher than ours. Lily is in a better place. We'll understand someday. The words felt hollow even as she spoke them; they changed nothing. By fall, Gail described herself as agnostic. By Christmas, she refused to bow her head for the dinner prayer. By the following spring, she was posting essays online dismantling the faith her mother had spent eighteen years carefully constructing.

Anna had done everything right. Youth group every Wednesday. Church every Sunday for twelve years. Summer camps. Mission trips.

Gail led worship for the high school ministry, memorized Scripture, wore a purity ring, and could present the gospel to anyone who asked. Her faith looked unshakeable. Yet, it shook loose in a single tragedy. When Anna finally sat across from her pastor, she could barely speak. "I protected her from everything. She never had to struggle with any of this." Her pastor leaned forward. "That's exactly why she's struggling now." Anna had built her daughter a greenhouse faith. Climate controlled. No harsh winds. No drought. No predators. Every condition optimized for comfort and growth. And like a greenhouse plant transplanted into an open field, Gail's faith couldn't survive its first real winter. This book argues that Anna's approach, though loving and heartbreakingly common, produced the opposite of what she intended. By eliminating stress from Gail's spiritual formation, she made her daughter's faith fragile. It looked vibrant. It performed beautifully in controlled conditions. But it had no capacity to handle pressure, uncertainty, or opposition.

Three Responses to Stress

Risk analyst and philosopher Nassim Nicholas Taleb spent decades asking a peculiar question: why do some systems collapse under pressure while others actually need pressure to thrive? His research identified three categories that change how Christians should think about faith formation.

Fragility: fragile things break under stress. Consider a wine glass. It's fragile. Drop it and it shatters. Handle it roughly and it chips. Fragile things require careful treatment. They need protection from shock, pressure, and volatility. Shipping fragile items means wrapping them in padding, placing them in sturdy boxes, and marking them with warning labels. The goal is to minimize stress and variation.

Resilience: resilient things withstand stress unchanged. Think about a rubber ball. It's resilient. Drop it and it bounces. Squeeze it and it returns to its original shape. Resilient things absorb stress without breaking. When pressure releases, they snap back. Resilience is better than fragility, but it's still essentially defensive. The resilient object survives stress without being fundamentally changed by it. Most discussions of faith operate within this framework. Christians ask whether someone's faith is strong enough to withstand trials or weak enough to break under pressure. They talk about building resilient faith that can endure hardship. They use metaphors of standing firm, holding fast, and remaining unshaken. These are biblical images and they matter. But they don't capture the full picture of how faith develops.

Antifragility: antifragile things require stress to grow stronger. Consider your immune system. It's not fragile or merely resilient. It's antifragile. When you encounter a pathogen, your immune system doesn't just survive the experience. It learns from it. It develops antibodies. It becomes stronger and more capable. The next time it meets that pathogen, it defeats it faster and more effectively. Stress doesn't just fail to break the immune system, stress improves it. Or consider your muscles. When you lift weights, you create tiny tears in muscle fibers. This sounds like damage, and in the immediate term, it is. But your body responds by building the muscle back stronger. The stress of lifting doesn't weaken the muscle. It's the mechanism by which muscles grow. This is antifragility: *the capacity to gain from disorder, to improve through stress, to grow stronger under pressure.* Antifragile things don't just resist harm. They need volatility and challenge to develop properly. Faith is designed to be antifragile. And treating it as fragile—protecting it from all stress—produces the very collapse that protection was meant to prevent.

The Fragility Trap

The fragility trap unfolds predictably. Parents love their children. They want to protect what they love. So they eliminate challenges. They sidestep hard questions. They insulate young believers from doubt. They engineer environments where nothing threatens faith. The intention is safety. The result is weakness. Consider what happens to the typical young Christian between graduation and age twenty-five. After years in controlled religious environments, the college freshman encounters professors who treat faith as primitive superstition. Intelligent, compassionate friends live without God and seem perfectly content. Sunday school answers cannot address adult questions about suffering, injustice, and doubt. News breaks about pastoral scandals and church failures that youth group never mentioned.

Some navigate this successfully. Many do not. Those who emerge with faith intact typically share a common history: somewhere along the way, they encountered difficulty inside their faith and wrestled through it. They raised hard questions and received honest engagement rather than deflection. They suffered and learned to bring pain to God rather than explain it away. They confronted the church's failures and chose Christ anyway. Their faith had been stressed. It grew back stronger. Those who abandon faith often share a different history: protection. Their parents and pastors shielded them from anything unsettling. Doubt was treated as dangerous rather than developmental. Hard questions met dismissal rather than exploration. Suffering prompted clichés rather than honest lament. The church's sins stayed hidden. These young believers entered adulthood with faith that had never been tested. And untested faith is not strong faith. It is faith waiting to shatter.

The Biblical Pattern

Scripture never promised believers a stress-free path to maturity. It promised the opposite. James opens his letter with a statement that should stop every overprotective Christian parent: "Count it all joy, my brothers, when you meet trials of various kinds, for you know that the testing of your faith produces steadfastness. And let steadfastness have its full effect, that you may be perfect and complete, lacking in nothing" (James 1:2-4). Note the logic. Trials test faith. Testing produces steadfastness. Steadfastness produces completeness. Remove trials, and the entire developmental chain breaks. James does not say believers should merely endure trials. He says to count them as joy because of what they produce. This is antifragility in biblical language. Peter makes the same point to persecuted Christians scattered across Asia Minor: "In this you rejoice, though now for a little while, if necessary, you have been grieved by various trials, so that the tested genuineness of your faith—more precious than gold that perishes though it is tested by fire—may be found to result in praise and glory and honor at the revelation of Jesus Christ" (1 Peter 1:6-7).

Gold does not become pure by being protected from fire. Gold becomes pure by passing through fire. The heat burns away impurities. What remains is stronger, more valuable, more genuine. Faith works the same way. The testing is not incidental to spiritual formation. It is essential to it. Paul traces the progression explicitly: "We rejoice in our sufferings, knowing that suffering produces endurance, and endurance produces character, and character produces hope, and hope does not put us to shame" (Romans 5:3-5). Suffering is not an obstacle to hope. Suffering is the path to hope. The sequence cannot be skipped. Even Jesus learned through suffering. Hebrews states it directly: "Although he was a son, he learned obedience through what he suffered" (Hebrews 5:8). If the incarnate Son of God developed through difficulty, what makes any believer think the path runs around hardship rather than through it. The author of Hebrews goes further, reframing divine discipline as evidence of love rather than abandonment: "For the Lord disciplines the one he loves, and chastises every son whom he receives... For the moment all discipline seems painful rather than pleasant, but later it yields the peaceful fruit of righteousness to those who have been trained by it" (Hebrews 12:6, 11). Discipline yields fruit. Training requires stress. Righteousness develops through difficulty that feels painful in the moment but produces peace over time. This is the biblical pattern. Protecting believers from all hardship does not honor this pattern. It contradicts it.

The Historical Pattern

Church history confirms what Scripture teaches. Christianity exploded under Roman persecution. Believers who risked execution for their faith developed conviction that comfortable religion cannot produce. Tertullian, writing around 200 AD, observed that the blood of martyrs became seed for the church. He was not being poetic. He was reporting what he witnessed: oppression spreading faith faster than safety ever could. Then Constantine legalized Christianity, and eventually made it the empire's official religion. When following Jesus cost nothing, faith grew shallow. The selection pressure that had filtered for genuine devotion disappeared. Nominal Christianity became possible, then common. This pattern echoes across centuries. The Huguenots maintained vibrant faith through massacres and exile. The underground church in China has multiplied for decades under Communist suppression. Believers in Iran risk imprisonment for house church gatherings and report remarkable growth. Meanwhile, comfortable Western Christianity produces young people who abandon faith at the first serious intellectual or emotional challenge. *Persecution, it turns out, is not the greatest threat to faith. Comfort is.*

The Path Forward

This book charts a different course for Christians who want to build faith that lasts. Not reckless exposure to every threat. Not abandonment of community, Scripture, or spiritual practices that genuinely strengthen and sustain. But intentional, thoughtful embrace of productive difficulty. Recognition that deep faith forms through struggle, not around it. The chapters ahead examine what this means in practice: How spiritual disciplines function as controlled stressors that build capacity rather than merely demonstrate piety. Why rapid repentance and honest confession develop stronger faith than hiding failure ever could. What it means to put skin in the game spiritually, moving beyond theoretical belief to costly obedience. How to raise children whose faith can withstand hostile classrooms, skeptical friends, and a post-Christian culture.

How to engage that culture strategically, in ways that sharpen conviction rather than erode it. And how to embrace the long view that trusts God's patient work across decades and generations rather than demanding immediate results. The church has always understood this.

The apostles embodied it. The martyrs demonstrated it. The desert fathers practiced it. The persecuted church lives it today. Somewhere along the way, in the comfort of climate-controlled sanctuaries and carefully curated youth programs, this understanding faded. Parents like Anna, wanting desperately to protect what they loved, accidentally produced the fragility they feared. Gail's story does not have to be the norm. Another way exists—an ancient way, a biblical way, a way that builds faith designed to grow stronger through the very pressures that shatter greenhouse belief. It's time to recover what comfortable Christianity forgot.

Chapter One

Beyond Resilience

Sarah grew up in a church that emphasized feeling good about God. The youth group focused on fun activities and positive messages. Bible studies highlighted encouraging verses. When doubt or questions arose, leaders quickly provided reassuring answers. The goal was to protect faith, to keep it safe from anything that might damage it. Sarah appreciated the care, but when she arrived at college, her faith lasted less than a semester. The problem wasn't that her church had taught her wrong theology. The problem was that they had treated her faith like something fragile, something that needed protection from stress. No one had prepared her for hostile professors, persuasive arguments against Christianity, or the social cost of standing apart from her peers. Her faith had been kept in a protective bubble, and when that bubble popped, the faith inside couldn't withstand the pressure.

Meanwhile, Sarah's roommate April had a different experience. April's church had encouraged questions and doubts. Her youth pastor didn't panic when teenagers challenged biblical teachings. Instead, he worked through objections carefully, admitted when he didn't have answers, and helped students learn to think critically about their faith. April's small group included tough conversations about suffering, injustice, and intellectual objections to Christianity. By the time she reached college, she had already wrestled with most of the arguments her professors presented. The opposition she encountered didn't weaken her faith. It deepened it. The difference between Sarah and April illustrates the difference between fragile faith and antifragile faith. But before we can understand antifragility, we need to recognize that most discussions about faith only acknowledge two categories: things that break and things that don't break.

Three Types of Faith

Jeremy and Kate had been married for twelve years when Jeremy lost his job. Not just any job, but a career he had built for fifteen years, gone in a single restructuring announcement. The financial pressure was immediate. They had a mortgage, two kids, and one income suddenly reduced to zero. Jeremy had grown up believing that if you follow God faithfully, life goes smoothly. His parents had enjoyed stable careers and comfortable lives. His church preached that blessing follows obedience. Now unemployed at forty, Jeremy felt betrayed. If God was good and he had been faithful, why was this happening? His faith had been built on the assumption that following Christ meant avoiding hardship. When hardship arrived anyway, the foundation cracked. Six months into unemployment, Jeremy stopped going to church. His faith had been fragile.

Kate's response was different, though she faced the same circumstances. She had also believed God would provide and protect. When Jeremy lost his job, her first response was like his: confusion, anger, and questioning. But Kate had a practice of memorizing Scripture. In the weeks after Jeremy's job loss, she found herself returning to verses she had learned years earlier. She prayed, often in tears, but she prayed. She reached out to friends from church, admitting her struggles and asking for prayer. The hardship tested her faith, bent it, stressed it. But it didn't break. She held on. After nine months, Jeremy found a new position, and Kate's faith returned to roughly where it had been before the crisis. Her faith had been resilient.

But consider a third response, embodied by their friend Darrel, who had faced his own job loss three years earlier. Darrel's unemployment had lasted fourteen months. During that time, he had learned things about God he never would have discovered in stability. He learned that God's presence mattered more than God's provision. He learned to trust when he couldn't see outcomes. He learned that prayer was not a vending machine but a relationship. He learned which parts of his identity were built on career success and which parts were built on Christ. When Darrel finally found work again, he wasn't the same person. His faith hadn't just survived the trial. It had grown through it. He understood Scripture more deeply. He prayed more honestly. He cared less about comfort and more about obedience. The stress had fundamentally changed him for the better. His faith had been antifragile. These three responses represent three types of faith:

Fragile faith breaks under pressure. It depends on favorable circumstances. It requires life to go according to expectations. When those expectations are violated, it shatters. This faith is characterized by conditional commitment: "I'll follow God if he gives me what I want." It mistakes blessing for the goal and comfort for spiritual health.

Resilient faith survives pressure. It holds firm during trials. It endures hardship without abandoning core beliefs. When circumstances improve, it returns to its previous state. This faith is characterized by determination: "I'll follow God no matter what happens." It sees trials as obstacles to overcome, tests to pass.

Antifragile faith grows through pressure. It doesn't just survive trials but is transformed by them. It emerges from difficulty stronger, deeper, and more mature. When circumstances improve, it doesn't return to its previous state because it has genuinely changed. This faith is characterized by expectation: "I'll follow God and become more like Christ through whatever he allows." It sees trials as opportunities for formation, tools for transformation.

The Biblical Pattern

This framework isn't imported onto Scripture. It's embedded in Scripture and into the central ethos of the Christian faith. Consider James 1:2-4: "*Count it all joy, my brothers, when you meet trials of various kinds, for you know that the testing of your faith produces steadfastness. And let steadfastness have its full effect, that you may be perfect and complete, lacking in nothing.*" James doesn't say trials might produce maturity if believers handle them correctly. He says testing will produce steadfastness and maturity. The Greek word for testing here (dokimion) refers to the process of proving something's quality through stress. Ancient metalworkers tested metal by heating it and hammering it. The stress revealed impurities and, when done properly, produced stronger metal. James uses this metaphor intentionally. Faith is tested not to see if it will break but to make it stronger. Notice the progression: trials test faith, testing produces steadfastness, steadfastness increases your capacity. This is antifragility. The trial isn't just something to survive. It's the mechanism of growth. Remove the trial and you remove the development.

Paul makes the same point in Romans 5:3-5: "*We rejoice in our sufferings, knowing that suffering produces endurance, and endurance produces character, and character produces hope, and hope does not put us to shame.*" Again, the progression is clear. Suffering isn't incidental to spiritual growth. It's instrumental to it. Peter echoes this theme: "*In this you rejoice, though now for a little while, if necessary, you have been grieved by various trials, so that the tested genuineness of your faith, more precious than gold that perishes though it is tested by fire, may be found to result in praise and glory and honor at the revelation of Jesus Christ*" (1 Peter 1:6-7). The trial reveals genuine faith, but more than that, it produces genuine faith. The biblical writers don't treat hardship as an unfortunate interruption to normal Christian life. They treat it as a normal part of Christian life and a necessary part of Christian growth. This makes sense only if the Christian faith is inherently antifragile.

How Antifragility Works

Consider how a tree develops. A tree grown in a greenhouse, protected from wind, grows quickly. It looks impressive. But its wood is weak. The trunk is thin. The roots are shallow. The first strong wind that hits it after it leaves the greenhouse will snap it. Now consider a tree grown in the wild, exposed to regular wind. Wind stresses the tree. It bends the trunk, forces the roots to dig deeper, and stimulates the production of stress wood that is denser and stronger. The wind doesn't harm the tree. The wind makes the tree stronger. A tree that has grown in the wind can withstand storms that would destroy the greenhouse tree. This is called thigmomorphogenesis: the developmental response of plants to mechanical stress. The stress isn't damage to overcome. It's a signal the tree needs to grow stronger. Remove the stress and you get a tall, weak tree. Provide appropriate stress and you get an antifragile tree.

Faith works the same way. Consider two believers, both raised in Christian homes, both taught sound doctrine. One grows up in a context where Christianity is socially acceptable, even advantageous. No one challenges his beliefs. His Christian identity costs him nothing. The other grows up in a context where following Christ means social marginalization. She faces mockery for her beliefs. She must defend her faith regularly. She pays a social cost for her Christian identity. Which believer will develop deeper faith? Not the one protected from challenge, but the one who has had to work through challenges. The first believer's faith may be correct, but it hasn't been tested. It's greenhouse faith. The second believer's faith has been stressed, questioned, and refined. It's wild-grown faith.

This explains a puzzling pattern in Christian history. The church has often grown fastest and strongest under persecution while stagnating or declining in comfort. In the first three centuries, Roman persecution produced explosive Christian growth. In the twentieth century, the underground church in China multiplied despite or perhaps because of Communist oppression. Meanwhile, comfortable Western Christianity has often produced nominal believers who abandon faith when it becomes inconvenient. The pattern repeats at the individual level. Christians who have weathered serious trials often show deeper maturity than those who haven't. The person who has wrestled with doubt and come through it typically has stronger faith than the person who has never questioned. The parent who has lost a child and clung to God through grief often knows God in ways that the parent of healthy children doesn't. The missionary who has sacrificed comfort for obedience usually demonstrates conviction that the comfortable church attender lacks. This isn't to say suffering itself produces maturity. Plenty of people become bitter through hardship. Plenty of trials destroy faith rather than develop it. Antifragility has limits and requirements. Not all stress produces growth. But the absence of stress consistently produces weakness.

The Problem with Protection

The instinct to protect faith is natural. Parents want to shield their children from doubt. Pastors want to create environments where believers feel safe. Churches want to provide refuge from a hostile culture. None of this is wrong in itself. The impulse comes from love. But protection, when it becomes the primary approach to spiritual formation, can produce the opposite of what it intends. Faith that has been shielded from all difficulty doesn't develop the capacity to handle difficulty when it inevitably arrives. Safety feels like care, but it can quietly cultivate fragility.

A better approach treats doubt as an opportunity. When the teenager asks hard questions, a mature believer works through them with her. They examine the questions seriously. They acknowledge when answers are complex or uncertain. They model how to think critically while maintaining faith. This feels riskier. The teenager might not like the answers. She might continue doubting. But she learns that faith can engage hard questions. She develops intellectual muscles. When she reaches college, she's prepared. The same pattern appears in how Christians often approach trials. When a fellow believer faces hardship, the instinct is to resolve it quickly. Pray for fast relief. Work to restore comfort. These aren't wrong impulses. Scripture calls believers to bear one another's burdens. But when all discomfort is treated as bad and all ease as good, something gets missed: God uses trials to develop character. A friend loses her job. Instead of immediately trying to fix the situation, what if the response included asking how God might use this time? What if prayer focused not just on quick reemployment but on spiritual growth through the process? What if the expectation was that the trial would produce maturity? This doesn't mean ignoring practical needs. It means recognizing that God's purposes often include formation through difficulty.

The Path Forward

Understanding antifragility changes how Christians approach faith at every level. For individuals, it means seeking spiritual growth through challenge rather than avoiding all discomfort. For parents, it means preparing children for trials rather than protecting them from all hardship. For churches, it means creating environments that stress faith appropriately rather than eliminating all spiritual tension. None of this means seeking suffering for its own sake. Antifragility isn't masochism. The goal isn't pain but growth. Just as a weightlifter chooses appropriate weights that stress muscles without breaking them, believers should seek challenges that develop faith without destroying it. A difference exists between beneficial stress and harmful trauma.

But the starting point is recognizing that stress isn't the enemy of faith. The absence of stress is the enemy of growth. A faith that never faces questions remains shallow. A believer who never experiences trials remains immature. A church that never encounters opposition remains weak. The chapters ahead explore how to build antifragile faith in practice. But first, this pattern must be understood in light of Christian history. Why has the church so often thrived under persecution and stagnated in comfort? What does two thousand years of Christian experience reveal about the relationship between pressure and growth? The next chapter examines this history.

Chapter Two

The Historical Pattern

In 177 AD, a mob in Lyons, France dragged Christians from their homes. The persecution started with public harassment, escalated to beatings, and ended with executions in the arena. Among the victims was Blandina, a slave woman who endured torture for days before being killed. The Roman governor assumed the brutality would terrify other Christians into recanting their faith. It did the opposite. Witnesses described how Blandina's courage under torture strengthened other believers. Her example inspired wavering Christians to stand firm. Even some pagans watching the executions began asking what kind of faith could produce such conviction. Within decades, the church in Lyons had grown larger than before the persecution. The attempt to crush Christianity made it stronger.

This wasn't an isolated incident. For the first three centuries of Christian history, the pattern repeated across the Roman Empire. Persecution broke individual Christians but strengthened the church. Violence killed believers but multiplied conversions. Every attempt to eliminate Christianity seemed to make it spread faster. The early church was antifragile at the systemic level, gaining from the disorder meant to destroy it. Then something unexpected happened. The persecution stopped. An emperor converted. Christianity became legal, then favored, then mandatory. And the faith that had thrived under opposition began to struggle under acceptance.

The Antifragile Early Church

When Jesus told his disciples they would face persecution, he wasn't speculating. He was describing the condition under which the church would grow. In the book of Acts, Luke records arrests, beatings, and executions starting almost immediately. Stephen's stoning in Acts 7 launched a persecution that scattered believers from Jerusalem. Luke writes, "*Those who were scattered went about preaching the word*" (Acts 8:4). The persecution meant to silence the gospel spread it instead. Paul's ministry followed the same pattern. In nearly every city he visited, he faced opposition. Thessalonica: driven out by a mob. Berea: pursued by hostile Jews from Thessalonica. Corinth: brought before the Roman tribunal. Ephesus: sparked a riot. Philippi: beaten and imprisoned. The book of Acts reads like a catalog of hostility. Yet churches multiplied throughout the Mediterranean world. Why didn't persecution work? Several factors made the early church antifragile:

Decentralization. The church had no headquarters, no single leader, no centralized authority that could be captured or destroyed. When persecution hit Jerusalem, believers scattered and planted churches elsewhere. When Paul was imprisoned, other preachers continued his work. When one congregation was destroyed, others remained. The distributed structure meant that attacks on one part strengthened other parts by dispersing people and spreading the gospel.

Selection effect. Being Christian in the first three centuries cost something. It might cost your job, your social standing, your property, or your life. This price filtered out superficial commitment. People didn't become Christians casually or for social advantage. Those who joined the church did so with conviction. This produced a core of committed believers who were willing to suffer for their faith.

Witness of martyrdom. The word "martyr" comes from the Greek word for witness. When Christians died rather than recant, they bore witness to the reality of their faith. Tertullian, writing around 200 AD, observed that "the blood of the martyrs is the seed of the church." He wasn't being poetic. He was describing what he saw: executions that were meant to deter people from Christianity often attracted them instead. The courage of martyrs raised questions that comfortable Christianity never would: What do these people know that makes them willing to die?

Practical love. The early church gained credibility through action. When plague hit ancient cities, pagans fled while Christians stayed to care for the sick. When natural disasters struck, Christians shared resources with neighbors. This practical love stood out in Roman society and attracted notice. Under persecution, this witness intensified. Christians loved their enemies, forgave their persecutors, and maintained community despite pressure. The contrast with Roman values was stark. By 300 AD, despite centuries of persecution, Christianity had spread throughout the empire. Estimates suggest 5 to 10 percent of the population identified as Christian. The faith had moved from a small sect to a significant religious movement. Persecution had failed to stop it.

The Constantine Shift

In 312 AD, Constantine defeated his rival Maxentius at the Milvian Bridge. Constantine attributed his victory to the Christian God and began favoring Christianity. The Edict of Milan in 313 made Christianity legal. By 380, under Emperor Theodosius, Christianity became the official religion of the empire. The persecution (from the Roman Empire) was over. This seemed like an unambiguous victory. Christians could worship freely. Church buildings multiplied. Bishops gained political influence. Resources flowed to Christian institutions. No more hiding, no more fear, no more martyrs. The church could finally flourish in peace. But, in some cases, something was lost. When Christianity became socially advantageous, people became Christians for the wrong reasons. Career advancement, political connections, and social acceptance motivated conversions. The price of discipleship dropped to nearly nothing. The selection effect that had filtered out casual commitment disappeared.

Church historian Kenneth Scott Latourette notes that as Christianity gained political power, "the moral quality of the average Christian declined." Bishops became politicians. Doctrinal disputes turned into power struggles backed by imperial force. Wealth and property created new temptations. The church that had been decentralized and grassroots became hierarchical and institutional. This isn't to romanticize persecution or claim Constantine's conversion was bad. Religious freedom matters. The end of state violence against Christians was genuinely good. But the shift from persecution to privilege revealed that much of the church's strength had come from pressure, not despite it. When the pressure released, weaknesses emerged that persecution had hidden or prevented.

Medieval Comfort and Corruption

By the medieval period, the church in Western Europe had become the dominant institution. It controlled vast wealth, owned significant land, and wielded political power. Becoming a priest could be a career move. Church positions were sometimes bought and sold. Some popes acted more like secular rulers than spiritual leaders. The corruption wasn't universal. Monasteries preserved learning. Saints demonstrated holiness. Missionaries spread the gospel to new regions. But the institutional church showed clear signs of fragility that comfort had produced. Consider these patterns:

Simony, the buying and selling of church offices, became common. When church positions offered wealth and power, they attracted people seeking wealth and power. The selection effect had reversed. Instead of filtering for commitment, church structures attracted ambition.

Theological stagnation. With Christianity culturally dominant, fewer believers thought deeply about their faith. The pressure that had forced early Christians to articulate and defend their beliefs was absent. Many Christians inherited faith as a cultural identity without understanding its content.

Moral decline among clergy. Some priests kept mistresses. Some bishops lived in luxury while their congregations starved. The gap between Christian teaching and Christian practice widened when the cost of hypocrisy dropped to nearly nothing.

Dependence on political power. The church relied on secular authorities to enforce orthodoxy and suppress heresy. This dependence made the church vulnerable. When political winds shifted, the church lacked the internal strength to stand independent of state support.

None of this means medieval Christianity was entirely corrupt or that all comfort produces decline. The point is simpler: the church that had been antifragile under persecution became fragile under privilege. It had adapted to one set of conditions and struggled when conditions changed.

Persecution and Renewal

The Reformation partly emerged from this fragility. When Martin Luther challenged church corruption, the response revealed how much the institutional church depended on political enforcement rather than persuasion. The church tried to silence Luther through traditional means: condemnation, excommunication, and calls for his execution. But the printing press had changed the landscape. Luther's ideas spread faster than authorities could suppress them. The ensuing religious conflicts were brutal. Catholics persecuted Protestants. Protestants persecuted Catholics. Both persecuted Anabaptists. But out of this turmoil came renewal. Churches that formed under persecution developed distinct characteristics:

Biblical focus. When you might die for your faith, you want to know what Scripture teaches. Reformation churches emphasized Bible study, translation into common languages, and theological education. The pressure to defend beliefs produced deeper biblical literacy.

Lay involvement. Persecution made hierarchical structures difficult. Reformed churches developed more distributed leadership. Believers learned to meet in homes, to teach each other, and to function without elaborate institutions. The stress produced flexibility.

Conviction over convenience. Joining a persecuted church meant accepting cost. This filtered for genuine commitment. The selection effect returned. Churches gained members who had weighed the cost and chosen Christ anyway.

Consider the Huguenots, French Protestants who faced severe persecution in the sixteenth and seventeenth centuries. Despite massacres, forced conversions, and exile, Huguenot churches maintained vibrant faith. When Louis XIV revoked religious toleration in 1685, thousands chose exile over recanting. They lost property, status, and homeland rather than compromise their faith. This wasn't fragile faith. This was faith that had been tested and proved strong.

The Modern Pattern

The same pattern appears in modern history. Consider three cases:

Soviet Union. When the Bolsheviks took power in 1917, they began systematic persecution of the church. They confiscated church property, executed clergy, sent believers to labor camps, and promoted atheism through education and propaganda. The institutional church collapsed. By 1939, only a handful of churches remained open in a country that had thousands before the revolution. Yet Christianity survived underground. Believers met in secret. They memorized Scripture because Bibles were scarce. They baptized converts at night in remote locations. Grandmothers taught grandchildren the faith despite risk. When the Soviet Union fell in 1991, observers expected to find a few elderly believers clinging to the remnants of faith. Instead, they found underground networks of committed Christians, particularly among young people who had never known religious freedom.

The seventy years of persecution had done what centuries of state support had failed to do: produce Christians who understood the cost of faith and chose it anyway. The selection effect had worked. Those who remained Christian under Soviet oppression were there because they believed, not because it was culturally expected or socially advantageous.

China. When Mao's Communist party took control in 1949, there were roughly one million Christians in China. The government expelled foreign missionaries, closed churches, imprisoned pastors, and actively persecuted believers during the Cultural Revolution. By Mao's death in 1976, institutional Christianity appeared nearly extinct. But the house church movement had grown underground. In homes and secret meetings, Chinese Christians studied Scripture, prayed, and made converts. These churches operated without seminaries, without buildings, without financial support, and without legal protection. They developed creative methods for discipleship and multiplication. Leaders faced constant risk of arrest.

Today, estimates of Chinese Christians range from 60 to 100 million. The exact number is uncertain because many worship in unregistered house churches. But even conservative estimates suggest growth from one million to 60 million in seventy years, mostly during periods of persecution. The Chinese church is one of the fastest-growing Christian movements in history, built not in freedom but under pressure.

Iran. After the Islamic Revolution in 1979, Iran became officially hostile to Christianity. Converting from Islam to Christianity became illegal, punishable by imprisonment or death. Churches faced strict government control. Evangelism was forbidden. Yet Christianity has grown, particularly among young Iranians disillusioned with the Islamic regime. House churches meet secretly. Believers use encrypted communications. Converts risk everything. By some estimates, Christianity in Iran is growing faster now than at any point in its history. The governmental opposition meant to eliminate Christianity has instead created conditions where faith grows stronger because it costs something.

The Western Contrast

Meanwhile, Christianity in Western Europe has declined dramatically. In countries where the church once held cultural dominance, attendance has dropped, church buildings have closed, and Christian identity has weakened. Britain, once a bastion of Christianity, now has more Muslims attending religious services than Anglicans. Scandinavian countries that were historically Christian now are among the most secular in the world. Many factors contribute to this decline: philosophical shifts, prosperity, individualism, and cultural change. But one factor stands out: Christianity became comfortable. In most of Western Europe, being Christian provides no social advantage. But it also creates no social cost. Faith became optional and socially neutral. The selection effect disappeared. People inherited Christian identity culturally without embracing Christian conviction personally.

When faith costs nothing, it often means nothing. When cultural Christianity faces challenges from secularism, it has few resources to draw on. It hasn't been tested. It hasn't had to defend itself intellectually. It hasn't required sacrifice. Like the greenhouse tree that hasn't experienced wind, it lacks the strength to withstand pressure. The contrast between growing churches in China and declining churches in Europe isn't about theology. Both contexts include Biblically faithful believers. The difference is environmental pressure. Chinese Christians face opposition that forces them to weigh the cost, think deeply about their faith, and develop resilient practices. European Christians often inherit a cultural identity that requires nothing and produces little conviction.

Understanding the Pattern

History reveals a consistent pattern: persecution tends to strengthen the church while comfort tends to weaken it. But this pattern requires careful interpretation. The point is not that persecution is always good or comfort is always bad. The goal is to understand how different pressures affect faith at the systemic level. Several mechanisms explain the pattern:

Selection. When faith costs something, people who become Christians do so with conviction. This creates a core of committed believers. When faith costs nothing, people drift into Christianity for cultural reasons and drift out when culture shifts.

Clarity. Opposition forces believers to understand and articulate their faith. Persecution removes ambiguity about what it means to follow Christ. Comfort allows vagueness and confusion about Christian identity.

Dependence on God. When believers can't rely on institutions, cultural support, or political power, they learn to depend on God. When those external supports are present, dependence on God becomes optional.

Community. Persecution strengthens bonds between believers because they need each other to survive. Comfort allows individualism because community becomes optional rather than essential.

Witness. Christians who suffer for their faith provide powerful testimony. Christians who experience no cost for their faith provide little contrast with surrounding culture.

This doesn't mean persecution should be sought. The history isn't prescriptive. It's descriptive. It shows us how antifragility works at the level of the church: opposition applies pressure that eliminates superficial faith while strengthening genuine commitment. Comfort removes pressure, which allows superficial faith to persist while genuine faith atrophies through lack of exercise.

Learning from History

What does this pattern teach us? First, Christians should expect trial and opposition as normal rather than exceptional. The New Testament promises that "*all who desire to live a godly life in Christ Jesus will be persecuted*" (2 Timothy 3:12). History confirms this. The unusual condition isn't opposition but widespread cultural acceptance. Second, institutional strength differs from individual spiritual strength. The medieval church was institutionally powerful but spiritually weak in many ways. The Chinese house church is institutionally fragile but spiritually vibrant. Christians often confuse these categories, thinking that large buildings, political influence, and cultural dominance indicate spiritual health. History suggests otherwise.

Third, believers should be cautious about using political power to advance Christian interests. When the church relies on state enforcement, it becomes fragile. It loses the capacity to persuade and the practice of suffering. It trades spiritual authority for temporal power, a trade that often impoverishes faith even when it appears to strengthen institutions. Fourth, difficulty filters commitment. Presenting faith as making life easier attracts people seeking ease. Presenting faith honestly as demanding and costly attracts people willing to pay the cost. The first approach fills churches with consumers. The second builds churches of disciples. Finally, Christians should pay attention to where the church is growing and why. The most vibrant movements today are often in contexts of pressure: house churches in China, underground churches in Iran, persecuted believers in parts of Africa and the Middle East. These movements offer lessons that comfortable Western churches need to learn.

The Path Forward

But persecution cannot be manufactured, nor should it be. The question is whether believers can develop the characteristics that pressure produces naturally: deep biblical conviction, commitment that weighs cost, community that goes beyond convenience, and dependence on

God rather than cultural support. Most Western Christians face no tribunals or execution threats. The surrounding culture may be increasingly hostile, but relative comfort remains the norm. If external pressure produces growth, what happens when circumstances provide none?

The answer lies in creating internal pressure through intentional practice. Throughout church history, believers have understood that spiritual growth requires deliberate challenge. They developed disciplines that function like a gymnasium for the soul, building capacity through voluntary discomfort. Fasting, solitude, confession, simplicity: these practices stress faith in controlled, beneficial ways. Such disciplines don't replace the refining work of external trials. But they prepare believers for trials when they come and prevent the atrophy that comfort produces when they don't. The same God who works through persecution also works through chosen discipline. Both involve stress that strengthens. One cannot be controlled. The other is chosen.

Chapter Three

The Spiritual Gymnasium

History shows that external pressure often strengthens faith while comfort weakens it. But most believers today face no persecution. If challenge produces growth, what happens when circumstances provide none? The answer lies in practices Christians have embraced for centuries: spiritual disciplines. These are not merely habits of devout believers or boxes to check for spiritual credibility. They function as voluntary stressors that build capacity the same way physical exercise builds strength. Fasting, solitude, confession, simplicity, and service create controlled difficulty that develops what comfort never could. This chapter examines how these ancient practices work and why the discomfort they produce is not an obstacle to growth but the very mechanism of it.

Boris joined a gym in January with typical New Year's resolution enthusiasm. His goal was simple: get in shape. He showed up the first day, looked at the equipment, and realized he had no idea what he was doing. A trainer explained the basics: muscles grow by being broken down through resistance training. You stress the muscle fibers, creating micro-tears. Your body repairs them stronger than before. No stress, no growth. Boris understood the principle but struggled with the practice. Lifting weights was uncomfortable. It required effort. It sometimes hurt. He could avoid all that discomfort by simply not going to the gym. Within three weeks, he had stopped going. The resistance that would have made him stronger felt like an obstacle to avoid.

Some Christians approach spiritual disciplines the same way. Most Christians understand that practices like prayer and solitude matter for spiritual growth. History confirms that believers across centuries have emphasized these disciplines. But when put into practice, discomfort follows. Prayer can feel dry. Fasting produces hunger. Solitude surfaces thoughts that would rather stay buried. So, the practices get abandoned. The discomfort gets treated as a problem rather than recognized as the mechanism of growth. Spiritual disciplines are controlled stressors. They put deliberate pressure on our spiritual lives in ways that produce maturity. Just as physical exercise stresses the body to make it stronger, spiritual disciplines stress our faith to make it deeper. They create the kind of beneficial difficulty that antifragile systems need to develop.

How Disciplines Function

Before examining specific disciplines, we need to understand how they work. Three principles explain their function:

Disciplines challenge default patterns. Most of us live on autopilot. We eat when hungry, speak when we have something to say, stay busy to avoid boredom, and seek comfort when uncomfortable. These patterns are natural, but they limit growth. Disciplines interrupt the patterns. Fasting challenges our relationship with food and comfort. Silence challenges our relationship with words and noise. Solitude challenges our relationship with people and distraction. By disrupting our defaults, disciplines reveal what controls us and create space for different patterns to develop.

Disciplines create focused attention. Normal life scatters our attention across dozens of demands. Work, family, entertainment, and responsibilities fragment our focus. Disciplines concentrate attention on God and spiritual reality. When you fast, hunger reminds you to pray. When you practice silence, the absence of words makes you aware of God's presence. When you serve others, you notice needs you normally overlook. This focused attention develops spiritual awareness that distraction prevents.

Disciplines build capacity through repetition. You can't develop strength by lifting weights once. You develop it through consistent practice over time. The same applies spiritually. One day of prayer won't transform your prayer life. Regular prayer over months and years will. One experience of fasting won't change your relationship with food and desire. Repeated fasting will. Disciplines work through accumulated practice, gradually increasing your spiritual capacity. These principles explain why disciplines feel difficult and why that difficulty matters. They're supposed to challenge you. The challenge is the point. Remove the challenge and you remove the growth mechanism.

Fasting: Learning Hunger

Paul writes that the Spirit produces self-control as fruit in believers' lives (Galatians 5:22-23). When you choose not to eat despite hunger, you practice saying no to physical desire. This practice strengthens your capacity to resist other desires: anger, lust, greed, pride. The muscle you build through fasting transfers to other areas. Fasting increases compassion. When you experience hunger voluntarily for a day, you gain small insight into what others experience involuntarily. The person who fasts regularly often becomes more generous, more aware of others' needs, more willing to share resources. The discipline creates empathy that comfort prevents. The early church practiced fasting regularly. Christians fasted on Wednesdays and Fridays. They fasted before major decisions. They fasted as preparation for baptism and ordination. The practice was normal, not exceptional. Many are unwilling to accept even minor, voluntary discomfort. This unwillingness keeps them weak.

Solitude and Silence: Confronting Ourselves

Brad's church hosted a silent retreat. Participants would spend twenty-four hours without speaking, phones, or other distractions. Just silence, solitude, and Scripture. Brad signed up, thinking it would be relaxing. He was wrong. The first few hours felt strange but manageable. Without his phone, Brad noticed how often he normally checked it. Without conversation, he became aware of how much energy he spent on social interaction. Without noise, he heard his own thoughts more clearly. Then it got hard. Memories surfaced that Brad had been avoiding. Anxieties he had been suppressing emerged. Questions about life direction he had been ignoring demanded attention. Without distractions, Brad had to face himself. It wasn't peaceful, it was uncomfortable. Several participants left early. Brad almost did. But he stayed.

By the end of twenty-four hours, something had shifted. The anxieties were still there, but Brad had brought them to God in prayer. The questions remained, but he had clarity about what decisions he needed to make. The memories still hurt, but he had started processing them honestly. The silence hadn't fixed anything, but it had created space for God to work. This is what solitude and silence do. They remove the distractions a person uses to avoid dealing with himself and God. Henri Nouwen wrote that "in solitude I get rid of my scaffolding." Modern life provides scaffolding made of noise, activity, relationships, and entertainment. The scaffolding holds people up, but it also prevents them from discovering whether they can stand without it. Solitude removes the scaffolding.

Jesus practiced solitude regularly. Mark records that "*rising very early in the morning, while it was still dark, he departed and went out to a desolated place, and there he prayed*" (Mark 1:35). This wasn't a one-time event. Luke writes that "*he would withdraw to desolate places and pray*" (Luke 5:16). Before major decisions, Jesus spent extended time alone. Before choosing the twelve disciples, he spent the night on a mountain in prayer (Luke 6:12). If Jesus needed solitude, every believer certainly does. But solitude surfaces what has been avoided. It reveals the state of the inner life that busyness masks. Many Christians stay busy partly to avoid this revelation. They fear what silence might expose.

The Desert Fathers understood this. In the fourth century, Christians fled to the Egyptian desert seeking God through solitude. They described battles with demons, temptations, and inner chaos that silence exposed. But they also described how extended solitude eventually produced peace, clarity, and intimacy with God. The path led through difficulty, not around it. Many modern Christians have abandoned these practices. Every moment fills with noise. Silence feels uncomfortable. Being alone feels threatening. This avoidance produces spiritual weakness. Believers who never practice solitude never develop the inner resources that solitude builds. When crisis forces them into isolation, they lack the capacity to process it well.

Simplicity: The Discipline of Less

Jesus taught about simplicity repeatedly. "*Do not lay up for yourselves treasures on earth*" (Matthew 6:19). "*You cannot serve God and money*" (Matthew 6:24). "*Take nothing for your journey*" (Luke 9:3). His disciples lived simply, depending on God's provision and others' generosity. Paul learned "*the secret of facing plenty and hunger, abundance and need*" (Philippians 4:12). Early Christians shared possessions and lived modestly. Modern consumer culture pushes the opposite direction. Modern consumer culture preaches that more is better, that accumulation equals success, that comfort and luxury are deserved. Christian culture has often absorbed these values. Churches build larger buildings. Believers accumulate more possessions and maintain packed schedules. Few stop to question whether any of this serves spiritual growth. Simplicity works as a discipline by removing safety nets. When you own less, you have less to fall back on. When you commit to less, you have less to hide behind. When you spend less, you depend more on God's provision. The removal creates vulnerability that forces dependence. This feels risky, which is why simplicity is a discipline. It requires choosing discomfort and vulnerability over security and control.

Confession: Exposing Failure

Dennis had been looking at pornography for years. He felt ashamed and resolved repeatedly to stop. Each resolution lasted a few days or weeks before he failed again. The cycle continued. The shame deepened. Dennis told no one. Then his small group started a study on James 5:16: "*Confess your sins to one another and pray for one another, that you may be healed.*" The leader asked if anyone wanted to confess specific struggles. Dennis felt the Holy Spirit prompting him. He was terrified. What would people think? Would they judge him? Would they tell others?

He confessed anyway. He told the group about his pornography use, his failed attempts to stop, and his shame. The room was quiet. Then another man said, "Me too." Then another. Four of the seven men in the group admitted similar struggles. They prayed for each other. They exchanged phone numbers with permission to call when tempted. Confession didn't fix Dennis's problem instantly. He still struggled. But several things changed. First, the shame lost its power. Once exposed, it couldn't control him the same way. Second, he had accountability. When tempted, he could text someone who knew his struggle. Third, he learned he wasn't alone. Other believers fought the same battle. Fourth, confession created honesty with God. He stopped pretending he had everything together.

Over time, Dennis's struggle diminished. Not because confession was magic, but because exposing sin to light reduced its power. Secrets thrive in darkness. Confession brings them into the open where they can be addressed. Most Christians avoid confession. They admit sin to God in private prayers but rarely confess to other believers. They fear judgment. They want to appear to have it together. They believe the lie that hiding sin protects them.

But James prescribes confession as medicine: "*...that you may be healed.*" Hiding doesn't protect believers. It makes them sick. Sin grows in secrecy. Confession exposes it to light where healing becomes possible.The early church practiced public confession. Believers confessed sins before the congregation. Church leaders prescribed periods of repentance. This seems harsh by modern standards. Contemporary culture values privacy and personal autonomy. But public confession served purposes that private confession cannot. It humbled pride. It created accountability. It normalized the reality that all believers struggle with sin. It made holiness a community project rather than individual effort. Christians today don't need to return to public confession, but recovering confession to trusted brothers and sisters remains essential. The practice functions as a discipline because it's uncomfortable. It requires vulnerability. It exposes failure.

Service: Challenging Self-Focus

Amanda served at a homeless shelter once a month. She helped prepare and serve meals. The first few times, she felt good about helping. Then the feeling wore off. Serving was inconvenient. It took time from her weekend. Some people she served were difficult or ungrateful. Amanda started finding excuses to skip her monthly commitment. Her friend Cori challenged her. "You're serving when you feel like it," Cori said. "That's not service. That's self-satisfaction. Real service costs something." Amanda was defensive at first. But Cori was right. Amanda had been serving on her terms, when convenient, as long as it made her feel good. When the cost increased, she quit.

Amanda committed to serve for six months without missing a shift, regardless of convenience or feelings. The discipline changed her. She learned names of people at the shelter. She heard their stories. She stopped seeing them as projects to help and started seeing them as people. She noticed needs she had overlooked. She became less focused on whether serving made her feel good and more focused on whether it helped people. Service functions as a discipline by decentering the self. Most of us naturally focus on our own needs, comfort, and preferences. Service forces attention outward. It requires putting others' needs ahead of our own convenience. When done consistently, it rewrites our default orientation from self-focus to other-focus. Jesus modeled this dramatically. He washed his disciples' feet, a task reserved for servants. He explained, "*If I then, your Lord and Teacher, have washed your feet, you also ought to wash one another's feet*" (John 13:14). He described his mission: "*The Son of Man came not to be served but to serve, and to give his life as a ransom for many*" (Mark 10:45). Paul instructs believers to "*do nothing from selfish ambition or conceit, but in humility count others more significant than yourselves*" (Philippians 2:3). He describes Jesus emptying himself and taking the form of a servant as the pattern Christians should follow.

But service is only a discipline if it costs something. Helping when convenient isn't service. Giving from surplus isn't sacrifice. Real service requires doing what a person would rather not do, spending time they would rather keep, using resources they would rather save. The cost is what makes it formative. Mother Teresa understood this. She required her sisters to serve the poorest of the poor. Not because helping the poor was more valuable than other ministry, but because serving people who couldn't repay or reward them would purify their motives. The sisters couldn't serve for recognition or reciprocity. They had to serve out of love for Christ expressed through love for the poor. Many churches have professionalized service. They hire staff to do ministry. Members write checks instead of serving personally. Programs require minimal personal involvement. These approaches have value, but they remove the formative power of direct, costly service. When someone else does the serving, the individual Christian misses the discipline.

The Modern Resistance

The disciplines—fasting, solitude, confession, simplicity, and service—share something in common: they're all uncomfortable. They all require choosing difficulty over ease. And in many cases, modern Christianity has largely abandoned them. Consider the contrast. Historic Christianity emphasized disciplines as central to spiritual formation. Desert Fathers practiced extreme solitude. Medieval monks followed rigorous schedules of prayer, work, and fasting. Reformers stressed the importance of regular spiritual practices. Puritan writers produced extensive guides to disciplines. For most of Christian history, practices like fasting, simplicity, and confession were normal expectations, not exceptional commitments.

Many Christians today gravitate toward comfort. They choose churches with better amenities. They prefer sermons that encourage rather than challenge. They fit spiritual practices around convenience. They embrace the message that faith makes life easier, not harder. Practices requiring discomfort become optional extras for the especially devoted. This pattern produces believers who lack spiritual capacity. They haven't developed the strength that disciplines build. When trials arrive, they have few resources to draw on. They haven't practiced depending on God because they've rarely experienced genuine need. They haven't built self-control because they've rarely denied themselves.

They haven't developed deep compassion because they've rarely served sacrificially. They remain weak precisely where disciplines would have made them strong. The situation resembles someone who never exercises complaining about being weak. The solution isn't mysterious. Exercise builds strength. But exercise requires discomfort. Anyone who avoids all discomfort will remain weak. No amount of wishing for strength will produce it without the work.

Starting the Practice: Building Antifragile Traits

How does a Christian recover disciplines in a culture that avoids discomfort? How does a believer build antifragile habits that strengthen faith? The answer is both simple and hard: start practicing. Choose specific disciplines, commit to them for defined periods, and push through the discomfort.

Start small. Don't try to fast for forty days if you've never fasted before. Skip one meal. Practice silence for an hour before attempting a day. Give away a few possessions before radically simplifying. The goal is to build capacity gradually, not to test your limits immediately.

Choose practices that address your specific weaknesses. If you struggle with self-control, try fasting. If you're constantly distracted, practice silence and solitude. If you're anxious about possessions, work on simplicity. If you hide sin, find someone to confess to. If you're self-focused, commit to regular service. Target the areas where you need growth.

Set clear commitments. Vague intentions like "I should fast more" rarely produce results. Specific plans like "I will fast every Wednesday for the next three months" create accountability. Write down your commitment. Tell someone about it. Create structure that makes following through easier.

Expect discomfort and push through it. The disciplines work precisely because they're difficult. If fasting feels easy, you're probably not doing it long enough. If solitude feels peaceful immediately, you're likely still distracted. If service costs nothing, you're not serving sacrificially. The discomfort is the signal that the discipline is working.

Find community. Disciplines practiced alone are easier to abandon. When others share your commitment, accountability increases. Small groups can practice disciplines together: fasting on the same day, sharing confessions, serving as a team. The mutual support makes sustaining the practice more likely.

Remember the purpose. Disciplines aren't about earning God's favor. They're about creating space for God to work. They're about building spiritual capacity. They're about training yourself to depend on God, resist temptation, notice needs, and live differently. The practices are means, not ends. They serve growth in Christ, which is the goal.

The Path Forward

Spiritual disciplines create controlled stress that builds capacity. But even when you practice them faithfully, you still fail. You still sin. You still make mistakes. The question is what you do with those failures. Some Christians treat failure as catastrophic, something to hide or deny. Others rationalize it away without genuine repentance. But there's a third approach: failing small, acknowledging quickly, and learning constantly. This pattern creates antifragile faith just as surely as spiritual disciplines do. In fact, the two work together. Disciplines prepare you to handle failure well. And handling failure well deepens the lessons disciplines teach. Both involve stress that produces growth when approached correctly. The difference is that disciplines are voluntary. Failures are inevitable. Which means learning to fail well isn't optional for developing strong faith. It's essential.

Chapter Four

Small Failures, Big Learning

Davis had been embezzling from his company for three years before anyone noticed. It started small: he rounded up expense reports, claimed reimbursement for personal purchases, padded his travel costs. Each time he got away with it, he took slightly more. By the time auditors discovered the problem, he had stolen over $80,000. He lost his job, faced criminal charges, and destroyed his reputation. Meanwhile, Davis's coworker Frank made a different kind of mistake. He submitted an expense report that included a personal dinner by accident. The next day, he realized his error and immediately told his manager. He repaid the $50, apologized, and implemented a system to keep personal and business expenses separate. His manager appreciated the honesty and the quick correction.

Both men made mistakes involving expense reports. But Davis's approach turned a small problem into a catastrophic failure, while Frank's approach turned a small mistake into a learning opportunity. The difference wasn't in their initial errors. It was in how quickly they acknowledged and corrected them. This principle applies to spiritual life as directly as it does to business ethics. Christians who quickly acknowledge sin, repent, and adjust develop stronger faith than those who hide failures, rationalize problems, or wait until small issues become large crises. Small failures, addressed quickly, produce growth. Small failures, ignored or hidden, accumulate into disasters.

The Mathematics of Failure

Systems can be fragile to large shocks but benefit from small shocks. A bank that never experiences any loan defaults becomes reckless because it has no feedback about which lending practices are risky. When the big crisis finally hits, the bank collapses. But a bank that experiences regular small loan defaults learns which practices work and which don't. The small failures teach lessons that prevent catastrophic failure. The same pattern appears across domains. A bridge that experiences no stress between inspections might develop hidden structural problems that cause it to collapse. A bridge that shows small signs of wear gets repaired and remains safe. A forest that never has small fires accumulates deadwood that eventually fuels a massive conflagration. A forest with regular small fires clears undergrowth and remains healthy. The key is that small failures provide information and correction opportunities that prevent large failures. But this only works if the failures are noticed, acknowledged, and addressed. Hidden or ignored small failures don't prevent disasters, they accumulate into them.

Consider two students learning to drive. The first student makes small mistakes regularly: drifts out of his lane, forgets to check mirrors, takes turns too fast. His instructor corrects each mistake immediately.

The student adjusts his technique. By the time he takes his driving test, he has made hundreds of small errors and received hundreds of corrections. He's a competent driver. The second student is more cautious. She avoids situations where she might make mistakes. She drives slowly, stays in familiar areas, and never attempts challenging maneuvers in practice. When she takes her driving test, she hasn't made many mistakes because she hasn't taken many risks. But she also hasn't learned to correct problems quickly. When an unexpected situation arises during the test, she doesn't know how to respond. She fails. The first student's many small failures made him antifragile. Each mistake provided information that improved his driving. The second student's avoidance of failure left her fragile. She had no practice correcting errors, so when errors happened, she couldn't handle them. Spiritual growth follows the same pattern. Christians who acknowledge and repent of small sins regularly develop spiritual health. Christians who avoid acknowledging sin until it becomes undeniable remain spiritually weak. The difference is in the feedback loop.

The Power of Quick Repentance

Lisa felt irritated with her husband most evenings. Small things bothered her: how he loaded the dishwasher, his comments about her day, the way he scrolled his phone during dinner. She snapped at him, spoke sarcastically, and created tension. Each evening, she told herself she'd do better tomorrow. But the pattern continued. One week, Lisa's Bible reading included James 4:17: "*Whoever knows the right thing to do and fails to do it, for him it is sin.*" The verse struck her. She knew being short with her husband was wrong. She knew it damaged their relationship. But she had been treating it as a personality quirk rather than sin.

That evening, when she felt irritation rising, Lisa stopped. She prayed silently, acknowledged her sinful attitude, and asked God to change her heart. Then she apologized to her husband. "I've been treating you badly. I'm sorry. I'm working on this." Her husband was surprised but gracious. The next evening, the irritation came back. Lisa repeated the process: immediate recognition, prayer, repentance, and if necessary, apology. She did this daily for weeks. Several things changed. First, the gap between feeling irritation and recognizing it as sin shrank. She caught herself faster. Second, apologizing became less difficult. The first few times felt humiliating. After a dozen times, it felt normal. Third, the irritation itself diminished. The habit of immediately addressing it gave it less room to grow. Fourth, her relationship with her husband improved dramatically. He saw her effort and softened his own responses.

Quick repentance worked because it created a tight feedback loop. Sin was acknowledged and addressed immediately rather than being allowed to fester. Each cycle of recognition and repentance made the next cycle easier and more natural. Lisa built a habit of dealing with sin quickly, which prevented small sins from becoming entrenched patterns. David writes in Psalm 32 about the cost of hiding sin: "*When I kept silent, my bones wasted away through my groaning all day long. For day and night your hand was heavy upon me; my strength was dried up as by the heat of summer*" (verses 3-4). Then he describes the relief of confession: "*I acknowledged my sin to you, and I did not cover my iniquity; I said, 'I will confess my transgressions to the LORD,' and you forgave the iniquity of my sin*" (verse 5). The Psalm captures the physical and spiritual toll of unconfessed sin and the freedom that comes with quick acknowledgment. The longer Dennis waited, the worse he felt. When he finally confessed, relief came immediately.

The lesson is clear: quick confession prevents accumulated spiritual damage.

Confession as Feedback

Kyron attended a men's group that practiced weekly confession. Each Monday morning, five men met for breakfast and shared their struggles from the previous week. They confessed specific sins: anger at their kids, lust, laziness, dishonesty, pride. They prayed for each other and offered accountability. Kyron found the practice uncomfortable at first. Admitting failure felt like weakness. But over time, he noticed patterns. He tended to look at pornography when stressed at work. He was short with his wife when he stayed up too late. He was impatient with his children when he skipped his morning prayer time. The weekly rhythm of confession helped him identify these connections. More importantly, knowing he would confess on Monday influenced his choices during the week. When tempted to look at pornography on Thursday, he thought about explaining it to the group on Monday. The anticipation of confession created a barrier to sin. Not because he feared judgment, but because confession made the sin real and concrete in a way that private rationalization didn't.

The group also provided feedback that Kyron couldn't generate alone. When he confessed the same sin multiple weeks in a row, someone would ask about patterns. "You mentioned work stress three times. What's happening there?" The question prompted Kyron to address root issues rather than just managing symptoms. When he struggled with the same temptation, someone would suggest practical strategies. "Can you delete that app from your phone?" The external perspective caught what Kyron missed on his own. Confession to others creates feedback that confession to God alone doesn't provide—not because God needs help, but because people do. When a believer confesses only to God in private, the believer controls the narrative. It's easy to rationalize, minimize, or avoid being specific. When that same believer confesses to another person, the sin must be articulated clearly. The confessor hears the words spoken aloud. The confessor faces another person's reaction. These elements make confession more powerful and more costly, which is precisely why it's more effective.

James prescribes mutual confession: "*Confess your sins to one another and pray for one another, that you may be healed*" (James 5:16). The confession is mutual because everyone sins. No one stands in judgment. Everyone participates in the vulnerability. This creates community based on shared brokenness rather than maintained appearances.

Accountability Structures

Stella struggled with spending. She bought things impulsively, used credit cards to manage cash flow problems, and avoided looking at her bank balance. Her debt grew slowly but steadily. She knew she needed to change but lacked the discipline to do it alone. She asked her friend Layla to serve as financial accountability. They met monthly. Stella brought her bank statements, credit card bills, and budget. Layla asked questions: "What's this $200 charge?" "Why did you buy that?" "Does this align with your goals?" The questions weren't judgmental. They were clarifying. They forced Stella to explain her choices out loud. The accountability changed Stella's behavior. Before buying something, she thought about explaining the purchase to Layla. Often, that thought was enough to stop the impulse. When she did make questionable purchases, she had to own them in their monthly meeting.

The combination of anticipation and explanation created powerful motivation to change.

After a year, Stella's debt was decreasing instead of growing. She had a working budget. She understood her spending triggers. The monthly accountability hadn't fixed everything, but it had interrupted the pattern of denial and rationalization that had enabled her destructive habits. Accountability works by adding external observation to internal motivation. Most people know what they should do. The problem isn't knowledge, it's follow-through. Accountability creates a structure that makes follow-through more likely by adding someone who notices, asks questions, and cares about outcomes. The early church built accountability into its structure. Believers met in homes, often daily. They knew each other's lives intimately. Hiding sin was difficult when you saw the same people constantly. This proximity created natural accountability that modern, large, anonymous church settings lack.

Paul's letters reflect this accountability culture. He instructs believers to "*...admonish the idle, encourage the fainthearted, help the weak...*" (1 Thessalonians 5:14). He tells the Galatians, "*If anyone is caught in any transgression, you who are spiritual should restore him in a spirit of gentleness*" (Galatians 6:1). These instructions assume close relationships where believers know each other well enough to notice problems and address them. Modern Christians often resist accountability. Many value privacy and autonomy. They prefer keeping others out of their decisions. They bristle at questions about their choices. This resistance stems from pride and from a culture that elevates individual freedom over community responsibility. But the resistance produces weakness. Without accountability, believers repeat the same failures indefinitely.

Transparent Community

Jack's church had a polished culture. Everyone dressed well, smiled widely, and shared prayer requests about distant relatives or vague "unspoken" needs. No one admitted real struggles. When asked how they were doing, people said "blessed" or "great." The unspoken rule was clear: look like you have it together. Jack struggled with depression but told no one. He maintained appearances on Sunday while battling dark thoughts during the week. His isolation deepened his depression. He believed he was the only Christian who felt this way. If others knew, they would judge him or question his faith.

Then Jack visited his friend's church in another city. During the service, someone shared a testimony about recovering from addiction. Others prayed aloud for specific sins they were battling: anxiety, anger, selfishness. A couple asked for prayer for their struggling marriage. The vulnerability shocked Jack. These people admitted failure publicly. After the service, Jack talked with his friend. "Doesn't that vulnerability make people uncomfortable?" he asked. "At first," his friend said. "But it's freeing. When someone admits they're struggling, others realize they're not alone. The honesty gives permission for everyone to be real. It's like we finally stopped pretending." Jack started attending a small group at the new church. He eventually shared about his depression. Instead of judgment, he found understanding. Three others in the group took medication for mental health issues. They compared notes on therapists and treatments. They prayed for each other specifically. The transparency didn't solve Jack's depression, but it ended his isolation and gave him support he desperately needed.

Transparent community is antifragile because it exposes problems early and addresses them collectively. When everyone pretends to be fine, problems grow in secret until they become crises. When people admit struggles openly, the community can respond while problems are still manageable. This requires safety. People won't be vulnerable if they expect judgment or gossip. Leaders must model transparency by admitting their own struggles. The community must demonstrate grace when people confess sin. This takes time to develop. Churches with cultures of image maintenance can't instantly become transparent. But they can start moving in that direction. Dietrich Bonhoeffer wrote about this in *Life Together*. He argued that Christian community is built not on spiritual strength but on common brokenness before God. "The person who loves their dream of Christian community more than the Christian community itself becomes a destroyer of that community even though their personal intentions may be ever so honest, earnest, and sacrificial." What Bonhoeffer meant is that insisting everyone maintain an image of spiritual success destroys real community. Real community forms when people are honest about failure. The dream of perfect Christians prevents the reality of growing Christians.

The Perfectionism Trap

Angela grew up in a church that emphasized holiness and victory over sin. The message she absorbed was that Christians shouldn't struggle. Temptation was normal, but sustained struggle indicated spiritual failure. Mature Christians had victory. Immature Christians struggled.

When Angela struggled with sin in her twenties, she concluded she must not be a mature Christian. So, she hid her struggles. She presented herself as victorious while privately battling the same sins repeatedly. The gap between her public image and private reality created intense shame. The shame made her less likely to seek help, which meant her struggles continued. By her thirties, Angela was exhausted from pretending. She finally confessed her long-term struggles to a mentor. The mentor's response surprised her: "That's normal. I've struggled with similar things my entire Christian life. Sanctification is lifelong. We don't achieve sinless perfection this side of heaven."

Angela felt enormous relief but also anger. Why hadn't anyone told her this before? Why had the church communicated that struggle meant failure? The perfectionist message had isolated her for years and prevented her from getting help she needed. Perfectionism produces fragility because it can't handle failure. If Christians aren't supposed to sin, then sin becomes a crisis that must be hidden. If maturity means victory over temptation, then ongoing temptation must be concealed. The hiding prevents the quick repentance and confession that would produce growth. A healthier framework acknowledges that Christians sin and should expect to. Not because sin is acceptable, but because believers are not yet glorified. Paul describes his own struggle with sin in Romans 7: "*I do not understand my own actions. For I do not do what I want, but I do the very thing I hate*" (verse 15). If Paul struggled, no Christian should be surprised to struggle as well.

This doesn't excuse sin or lower standards. It recognizes reality. Christians are simultaneously justified and being sanctified. They are declared righteous in Christ while still being transformed into Christ's likeness. That transformation includes repeatedly failing, repenting, and growing. Progress isn't measured by absence of sin but by quicker recognition and repentance of sin. When churches communicate that Christians shouldn't struggle, they create cultures where people hide rather than confess. When churches communicate that struggle is normal and confession is expected, they create cultures where people can be honest and receive help.

Learning Systems

Companies that never make mistakes are usually companies that aren't innovating. They're playing it safe, doing what's proven, avoiding risk. Companies that make small mistakes regularly and learn from them often outcompete their more cautious competitors. The key is failing fast, learning quickly, and adjusting rapidly. Amazon exemplifies this approach. Jeff Bezos has said, "Failure and invention are inseparable twins." Amazon has launched countless products and services that failed. But each failure provided information that informed the next attempt. The Fire Phone flopped, but what Amazon learned contributed to Echo's success. The willingness to fail publicly and often has made Amazon adaptable and antifragile.

Contrast this with companies that avoid all risk and make no mistakes for years. When the market shifts or technology changes, they can't adapt because they haven't practiced learning from failure. They're fragile precisely because they've avoided the small failures that would have made them antifragile. Spiritual life works similarly. Christians who regularly acknowledge small sins, repent quickly, and adjust their behavior are learning systems. They're getting feedback about what works and what doesn't. They're developing the habit of course correction. When bigger temptations or trials come, they have practiced responses. Christians who avoid acknowledging sin until it becomes undeniable aren't learning systems. They're rigid systems that break under pressure. They haven't developed the habit of recognizing and addressing problems early. When major sin or crisis hits, they lack the reflexes to handle it well. This explains why some Christians who appear to be doing well spiritually fall into major sin while others who have struggled visibly for years remain stable. The visible strugglers have been failing small, repenting quickly, and learning constantly. They've built strong habits of confession and correction. The seemingly successful ones may have been hiding struggles, avoiding accountability, and not learning from mistakes. When crisis comes, the strugglers have resources to draw on. The successful ones don't.

The Modern Avoidance

Contemporary Christianity has often adopted therapeutic language that softens the reality of sin. Sin becomes "mistakes," "poor choices," or "struggles." Teaching emphasizes God's unconditional love while downplaying repentance. Messages focus on self-esteem and feeling good. These emphases contain truth, but they can create an environment where sin isn't taken seriously enough to be confessed specifically and repeatedly. The result is Christians who don't develop strong habits of repentance. They acknowledge sin in general terms but rarely in specific ones. They confess to God in private but not to others in community. They avoid the discomfort of specific, repeated confession and miss the growth it produces.

The early church operated differently. New believers learned specific lists of sins to avoid. Confession was specific and sometimes public. Church discipline addressed persistent sin directly. Repentance meant turning from sin toward righteousness, not merely feeling sorry. The emphasis fell on transformation, not comfort. Recovering every first-century practice isn't the goal. But recovering the reality that sin is serious, confession is necessary, and repentance must be specific and repeated—this matters. The modern softening of sin hasn't produced holiness. It has produced Christians comfortable with ongoing sin because they've lost the category of repentance.

Practical Steps

How can believers build cultures and habits where small failures produce learning? Several practices help:

Develop a personal repentance practice. Daily examination of conscience is an old Christian discipline. Before bed, review the day and confess specific sins to God. Don't settle for general acknowledgment. Name the sin specifically. Acknowledge the harm it caused. Ask for forgiveness. Plan how to avoid it tomorrow. This daily practice creates a tight feedback loop between sin and repentance.

Find a confession partner or group. Identify someone you trust or join a small group committed to mutual confession. Meet regularly, weekly if possible. Share specific struggles. Ask for prayer and accountability. The consistent rhythm matters more than the perfection of practice.

Make amends quickly. When you sin against someone, apologize as soon as you recognize the offense. Don't wait for them to bring it up. Don't let it fester. Quick apology mirrors quick repentance and prevents relational debt from accumulating.

Track patterns. Keep a list of sins you confess repeatedly. Patterns reveal root issues. If you confess the same sin weekly for months, something deeper needs addressing. Use the pattern data to identify triggers, underlying motivations, and necessary changes.

Celebrate repentance, not just victory. Churches often celebrate when someone overcomes sin but rarely celebrate when someone confesses sin. Both deserve celebration. The person who acknowledges failure and repents demonstrates spiritual health. Make space in community life to honor honest confession, not just successful resistance to temptation.

Teach children to fail well. Parents often protect children from failure or shame them for it. Neither approach teaches healthy repentance. When a child fails, help them acknowledge it, understand consequences, make it right, and move forward. Model this by admitting your own failures to your children. Let them see you apologize, repent, and grow.

The Foundation of Growth

The capacity to fail small, acknowledge quickly, and learn constantly is fundamental to antifragile faith. It's the mechanism by which believers grow in holiness. Without it, they stagnate. With it, they develop. This capacity doesn't exist in isolation. It requires community that supports transparency rather than demanding perfection. The perfectionism that hides struggles, the isolation that avoids accountability, the pride that refuses confession—these prevent the rapid feedback loops that produce growth. When communities create environments where failure can be acknowledged safely, they create environments where transformation actually happens. The practices described in this chapter aren't complicated. Daily examination of conscience. Quick confession when sin surfaces. Accountability relationships that ask hard questions. Communities that celebrate repentance rather than demanding flawless performance. None of this requires special training or unusual circumstances. It requires only the willingness to be honest about who a person is and who they're becoming.

The Path Forward

But there's a prior question. Does a Christian's faith actually govern life enough to produce failures worth learning from? Quick repentance only matters when a believer attempts obedience costly enough to risk failure. Confession only serves growth when someone lives in ways that require genuine accountability. The learning system described above assumes something is actually at stake. This raises an uncomfortable possibility. Some Christians experience few spiritual failures not because they've achieved holiness but because they've attempted nothing difficult. Their faith remains safely theoretical, never tested because never applied. They agree with Christian doctrine without letting it disrupt their finances, their reputation, their comfort, or their relationships. A person cannot fail at a faith they've never really practiced. The question isn't just whether believers repent quickly when they fall short. The question is whether they've invested enough in following Christ for falling short to be possible. Do they have skin in the game?

Chapter Five

Skin in the Game

Robert attended church every Sunday for twenty years. He knew theology. He could articulate the gospel. He agreed with his church's doctrinal statement. He described himself as a committed Christian. But his life looked identical to his non-Christian neighbors: same financial priorities, same entertainment choices, same career ambitions, same response to difficulty. His Christianity cost him nothing and changed nothing. It was a belief system he agreed with, not a life he lived. Meanwhile, his coworker Maria also identified as Christian. But her life looked different. She gave away 10 percent of her income, which meant living more modestly than her salary allowed. She volunteered at a homeless shelter weekly, which consumed her Saturday mornings. She had turned down a promotion that would have required compromising her ethics. She was known at work for honesty that sometimes created awkwardness. Her faith cost her money, time, career advancement, and social ease. It wasn't just something she believed. It was something she staked her life on.

Nassim Taleb emphasizes the principle of skin in the game: people who bear the consequences of their decisions make better decisions than those who don't. A pilot who flies the plane makes different safety decisions than a designer who stays on the ground. An executive whose wealth is tied to company stock makes different choices than one whose compensation is guaranteed regardless of performance. When you have skin in the game, you have something to lose. This concentrates your attention, sharpens your judgment, and reveals what you believe. Talk is cheap when consequences are abstract. Talk becomes meaningful when consequences are personal. Christianity is meant to involve total skin in the game. Jesus said, "*Whoever does not take his cross and follow me is not worthy of me. Whoever finds his life will lose it, and whoever loses his life for my sake will find it*" (Matthew 10:38-39). Following Christ was never meant to be theoretical. It was meant to be the fundamental stake that determines everything else.

Theoretical vs. Lived Faith

James addresses this distinction directly: "*What good is it, my brothers, if someone says he has faith but does not have works? Can that faith save him? If a brother or sister is poorly clothed and lacking in daily food, and one of you says to them, 'Go in peace, be warmed and filled,' without giving them the things needed for the body, what good is that? So also faith by itself, if it does not have works, is dead*" (James 2:14-17). James isn't saying works earn salvation. He's saying genuine faith produces works. Faith that produces nothing, that costs nothing, that changes nothing, isn't faith. It's agreement with certain propositions. Real faith stakes everything on Christ, which means it affects everything about how you live.

Consider two people who both say they believe the Bible is God's word. The first reads it occasionally, when convenient. The second organizes her life around studying and obeying it. Both claim the same belief. But only the second has skin in the game. Only the second has staked her life on the belief being true. The first person's belief is theoretical. The second person's belief is lived. This distinction appears throughout life. Many people theoretically believe exercise is important. Few organize their schedules around exercising daily. Many people theoretically believe relationships matter more than careers. Few sacrifice career advancement for relationships. The gap between theoretical and lived belief reveals what people value versus what they claim to value.

"Theoretical" Christianity is fragile because it has no roots. When pressure comes, when following Christ becomes costly, theoretical Christians abandon their beliefs because those beliefs never governed their lives anyway. They were ideas, not commitments. Ideas change easily because they cost nothing. However, "lived" Christianity is antifragile because it's been tested through cost. When you've already sacrificed for your faith, further sacrifice feels consistent rather than catastrophic. When your life is organized around Christ, pressure that forces you to choose between Christ and comfort reinforces rather than challenges your existing pattern. You've already chosen Christ over comfort repeatedly. One more choice follows the established direction.

The Cost of Discipleship

Dietrich Bonhoeffer distinguished between cheap grace and costly grace. Cheap grace is "the preaching of forgiveness without requiring repentance, baptism without church discipline, Communion without confession, absolution without personal confession. Cheap grace is grace without discipleship, grace without the cross, grace without Jesus Christ." Costly grace is "the gospel which must be sought again and again, the gift which must be asked for, the door at which a man must knock. Such grace is costly because it calls us to follow, and it is grace because it calls us to follow Jesus Christ. It is costly because it costs a man his life, and it is grace because it gives a man the only true life." Bonhoeffer wrote this in Nazi Germany. When he wrote about costly grace, he knew what he was describing. Following Christ there meant potential arrest, imprisonment, and death. Bonhoeffer chose to return to Germany from safety in America because his faith had skin in the game. It wasn't abstract theology. It was lived commitment. He was executed by the Nazis in 1945, weeks before the war ended.

Bonhoeffer's life illustrates what discipleship means when it costs something. Most Western Christians will never face the stakes Bonhoeffer faced. But the principle remains: faith that costs nothing is weak faith. Faith that costs something is strong faith. Not because suffering is inherently valuable, but because willingness to suffer reveals genuine conviction. Jesus stated the cost clearly: "*If anyone would come after me, let him deny himself and take up his cross and follow me*" (Mark 8:34). Taking up your cross isn't a metaphor for minor inconvenience. In the first century, crosses meant execution. Jesus was telling his followers that discipleship might cost them everything, including their lives. That's maximum skin in the game. The early disciples understood. They left occupations to follow Jesus. They faced rejection from families. They were beaten, imprisoned, and killed. Following Christ wasn't safe or comfortable. It was costly. That cost filtered out casual interest and reinforced genuine commitment.

Financial Skin in the Game

Dave and Susan made good money. Combined household income was $180,000. They lived comfortably: nice house, new cars, annual vacations, retirement savings. They attended church regularly and gave 3 percent of their income. They believed in generosity and tithing, but they also had financial goals and obligations. Giving more would mean adjusting their lifestyle, and they had worked hard to achieve their standard of living. When their church launched a building campaign, Dave and Susan pledged $500 over three years. It felt generous. But they didn't have to change anything to fulfill it. The pledge came from margin in their budget, not from sacrifice.

Their friends Tom and Amy made similar income but gave 20 percent. They lived in a smaller house than they could afford. They drove older cars. They took modest vacations. Their retirement savings were lower than financial advisors recommended. These weren't hardships exactly, but they were choices. Tom and Amy had decided their money belonged to God, which meant using it for his purposes rather than maximum comfort and security. When the building campaign launched, Tom and Amy pledged $15,000 over three years. They calculated carefully. They would need to reduce their already modest spending and postpone replacing their aging car. The pledge would require ongoing sacrifice. They prayed about it extensively before committing.

Both couples said they believed in generosity. But Tom and Amy had financial skin in the game. Their giving cost them something tangible. They had subordinated their financial decisions to their faith. Dave and Susan's giving was theoretical. It affirmed a principle without affecting their lifestyle. Jesus watched people give at the temple and pointed out a widow who gave two small coins: "*Truly, I say to you, this poor widow has put in more than all of them. For they all contributed out of their abundance, but she out of her poverty put in all she had to live on*" (Luke 21:3-4). Jesus measured giving not by amount but by cost. The widow gave more because it cost her more. She had skin in the game. Paul commends the Macedonian churches: "*In a severe test of affliction, their abundance of joy and their extreme poverty have overflowed in a wealth of generosity on their part. For they gave according to their means, as I can testify, and beyond their means, of their own accord*" (2 Corinthians 8:2-3). Giving beyond their means indicates sacrifice. The Macedonians had skin in the game. Modern Christianity has often made peace with wealth. Some Christians have embraced the teaching that God wants to bless them financially. Churches build expensive buildings and justify them as honoring God. Comfortable believers rarely hear challenges to give sacrificially. When financial skin is removed from the game, faith becomes more comfortable and more superficial.

Reputational Skin in the Game

Jessica worked in marketing at a pharmaceutical company. She was good at her job and positioned for promotion. Her team was developing a campaign for a new medication. As Jessica reviewed the data, she realized the campaign emphasized benefits while downplaying significant side effects. The messaging was technically legal but misleading. People who saw the ads would form an incomplete picture of the medication's risks. Jessica faced a choice. She could say nothing, the campaign would proceed, and her career would advance. Or she could object, which would create tension with her boss, delay the campaign, and possibly cost her the promotion.

Jessica prayed about it, discussed it with her husband, and decided to speak up. She drafted a memo explaining her concerns and suggesting changes to make the messaging more balanced. Her boss was annoyed. The team had to revise their work. The campaign launch was delayed. Jessica's next performance review was less positive than previous ones. She didn't get the promotion. A year later, the medication's side effects became a public relations problem. People who had taken it based on the original campaign felt misled. The company faced lawsuits. Jessica's boss remembered her early warnings. Eventually, Jessica was promoted, partly because she had demonstrated integrity when it was costly.

But even if the promotion had never come, Jessica had done what she believed was right. She had reputational skin in the game. She risked professional consequences because her faith informed her ethics. Her Christianity wasn't compartmentalized as a private belief. It governed her professional decisions. Daniel faced a similar situation in ancient Babylon. King Nebuchadnezzar commanded everyone to bow to a golden statue. Refusal meant death in a furnace. Daniel's friends Shadrach, Meshach, and Abednego refused. They told the king, "*If this be so, our God whom we serve is able to deliver us from the burning fiery furnace, and he will deliver us out of your hand, O king. But if not, be it known to you, O king, that we will not serve your gods or worship the golden image that you have set up*" (Daniel 3:17-18).

They had maximum skin in the game: their lives. Their faith wasn't theoretical. They staked everything on it being true, even when obedience meant probable death. God delivered them miraculously, but they had been willing to die either way. That willingness revealed the depth of their faith. Most Western Christians won't face execution for their faith. But smaller reputational costs present themselves regularly: the cost of being known as a Christian at work, the cost of explaining why certain activities are off-limits, the cost of inviting someone to church, the cost of defending unpopular Christian positions. These aren't trivial in a culture that increasingly views Christianity with skepticism. The question is whether a believer is willing to bear these costs. Faith that can be known only inside church buildings and must be hidden everywhere else lacks reputational skin in the game. It functions as a private preference that costs nothing publicly. That kind of faith is fragile because it has never been tested by cost.

Relational Skin in the Game

Eric's father was dying. They had never been close. His father was difficult, critical, and emotionally distant. Eric had moved across the country partly to escape their toxic relationship. He visited once a year out of obligation, not affection. When his father's cancer reached its final stages, Eric faced a choice. He could maintain the distance, visit for the funeral, and feel relief when it ended. Or he could move home for the final months to care for his father. Moving home would mean leaving his job, pulling his kids from school, and spending months caring for someone who had never cared well for him. Eric's pastor reminded him of Jesus's teaching: "*Love your enemies and pray for those who persecute you*" (Matthew 5:44). If Eric couldn't love a dying father who had failed him, could he claim to love God whom he'd never seen? Eric's Christianity would remain theoretical if he loved only people who loved him back.

Eric moved home. The next four months were harder than he expected. His father remained difficult, rarely grateful, sometimes mean. But Eric served him anyway: managing medications, helping with physical needs, handling logistics. He prayed for his father daily, asking God to soften both their hearts. Two weeks before his father died, something shifted. His father apologized for his failures as a parent. They had conversations they'd never had before. Eric's father expressed faith in Christ for the first time. He died peacefully with Eric holding his hand. Eric's faith cost him four months of his life, professional setbacks, and enormous emotional labor. But it was genuine faith, faith with skin in the game. He had sacrificed comfort to obey Christ's command to love. The obedience had required staking something real on his beliefs being true.

Paul writes about relational skin in the game: "*Owe no one anything, except to love each other, for the one who loves another has fulfilled the law*" (Romans 13:8). Love isn't a feeling. It's a commitment that costs something. You love people by sacrificing time, resources, and comfort for their good. That sacrifice puts skin in the game. You've invested in the relationship in ways that theoretical love never requires. Jesus modeled maximum relational skin in the game. He left heaven for earth, comfort for hardship, glory for humiliation. He served people who rejected him. He died for people who hated him. The cross represents total skin in the game: Christ staked everything on loving us, even when that love cost him his life.

Intellectual Skin in the Game

Melanie taught biology at a state university. She was a Christian who believed God created the world, but she taught evolutionary theory because that's what the curriculum required. She compartmentalized her faith and her profession. At church, she affirmed creation. In the classroom, she taught evolution without qualification. She never discussed how she integrated the two or whether she'd examined the tensions between them. Meanwhile, her colleague Lorenzo also believed in God and taught biology. But Lorenzo had wrestled intellectually with how his faith and his science related. He had read extensively on both sides. He could articulate why he believed God created through evolutionary processes and where he saw limitations in materialistic explanations. He occasionally mentioned these perspectives to interested students, not as dogma but as his own intellectual journey. Both were Christians teaching biology. But Lorenzo had intellectual skin in the game. He had done the hard work of thinking through apparent contradictions. He was willing to discuss his beliefs in an academic environment where they might be challenged or mocked. His faith wasn't compartmentalized from his intellect. He had integrated them, even when that integration was messy and incomplete.

Paul had intellectual skin in the game. He debated philosophers in Athens (Acts 17). He reasoned with Jews in synagogues, showing from Scripture that Jesus was the Messiah. He wrote letters with complex theological arguments. He engaged intellectually with objections to Christianity. His faith wasn't anti-intellectual or separate from reason. It involved his whole mind, even when that meant wrestling with hard questions. Many Christians avoid intellectual engagement with their faith. They separate belief from reason, trusting faith in the religious sphere while trusting reason in the professional and academic spheres. This compartmentalization protects faith from questions, but it also makes faith fragile. When intellectual challenges arise, compartmentalized faith has no resources to respond. Faith with intellectual skin in the game involves thinking seriously about what you believe and why. It means reading books that challenge your views. It means engaging with objections rather than dismissing them. It means being willing to change your mind when evidence warrants. This feels risky because it exposes faith to potential defeat. But it also strengthens faith by forcing it to prove it can withstand scrutiny.

The Selection Effect

When following Christ costs something, it filters who follows. This is the selection effect we've discussed before. When Christianity is culturally advantageous, people become Christians for wrong reasons. When Christianity is costly, people become Christians only if they're genuinely convinced it's true. In the early church, becoming Christian meant potential persecution, social rejection, and economic hardship. The cost filtered out casual interest. People who became Christians did so with conviction because the decision came with stakes. They had skin in the game from the moment of conversion.

In medieval Europe, being Christian was culturally expected and often legally required. The cost of Christianity dropped to nearly nothing. People became Christian because everyone was Christian. Faith became cultural identity rather than personal conviction. The selection effect reversed: Christianity attracted conformists rather than filtering for conviction. Modern Western Christianity operates somewhere between these extremes. Being Christian isn't culturally mandatory, but it isn't overtly costly either. This produces mixed results. Some Christians have genuine conviction. Others have inherited cultural identity. Without clear cost, the difference isn't immediately apparent.

The test comes under pressure. When following Christ requires sacrifice, cultural Christians drift away. Convinced Christians remain and often strengthen. The pressure doesn't create the difference. It reveals it. Those with skin in the game stay invested. Those without skin in the game exit when the game stops being fun. This explains a pattern in Christian history: churches grow stronger under persecution not because persecution is good, but because persecution filters for genuine faith. The cost removes nominal commitment and reinforces actual commitment. The church becomes smaller but more devoted. That devoted core often evangelizes more effectively than a large nominal church because their faith has substance born from sacrifice.

Risk and Faith Development

Michael had been a Christian for fifteen years but felt stagnant spiritually. He attended church, read Scripture occasionally, and prayed before meals. But his faith felt routine. Nothing was growing. His pastor challenged him to take a risk for his faith. What would it look like to stake something on Christ? Michael thought about it and realized he had insulated his faith from all risk. He gave money he wouldn't miss. He volunteered when convenient. He shared his faith only in safe contexts. Nothing about his Christianity cost him anything significant. Michael decided to volunteer at a prison ministry. He was scared. Prisons felt dangerous. He didn't know what to say to inmates. The time commitment was significant. But he committed to six months.

The experience changed him. He met men whose faith had been forged through genuine suffering. He heard stories of transformation that his comfortable church rarely produced. He learned to share his faith simply and directly because prisoners asked hard questions. He discovered that serving people society had rejected was both harder and more meaningful than serving people who could reciprocate. After six months, Michael's faith felt alive again. Not because prison ministry was magic, but because he had risked something for Christ. He had put skin in the game. The risk had required depending on God in ways that safe Christianity never demanded. His faith had grown through the stress of costing him something.

This is how antifragile faith develops. Faith that never risks anything remains weak. Faith that risks and sees God prove faithful grows stronger. Each act of costly obedience builds capacity for the next. You learn that God is trustworthy not through theoretical belief but through staking something on that belief and finding it reliable. The staking is what makes the difference. You can read about God's faithfulness for decades without growing much. But when you risk your reputation, your resources, or your comfort based on God's faithfulness, and he proves faithful, your trust deepens in ways reading never produces. The risk creates the growth.

The Modern Avoidance of Cost

Contemporary Christianity has often minimized cost. Churches promote faith as making life better, not harder. Sermons emphasize benefits: peace, purpose, community, and blessing. The harder teachings get downplayed: taking up crosses, dying to self, suffering for righteousness. The appeal is to try Christianity without fear of what it might cost. This strategy fills churches, but it produces consumers rather than disciples. People arrive expecting benefits without sacrifice, comfort without cost, blessing without obedience. When Christianity turns out to require something, many feel betrayed or misled. They signed up for one thing and got another.

A more honest approach would present Christianity as Jesus did: as the most important commitment anyone will ever make, the one that determines everything else, the one that might cost everything but is worth more than anything. This approach might attract fewer people initially. But it would attract the right people: those willing to stake their lives on Christ being true. Jesus never hid the cost. He told would-be disciples to weigh the cost before following (Luke 14:28). He said following him might divide families (Matthew 10:35-37). He warned that the world would hate his followers as it hated him (John 15:18-19). He promised suffering, not ease (John 16:33). This honesty filtered out casual interest and attracted devoted followers. Modern Christianity would benefit from recovering this honesty. Not to scare people away, but because genuine faith requires skin in the game. Faith that costs nothing develops weakly. Faith that costs something develops strongly. Strong Christians emerge from contexts where following Christ costs something.

Practical Steps Toward Skin in the Game

How do Christians develop faith with real stakes? Several practices help:

Make financial commitments that require sacrifice. Don't give from surplus. Give from substance. Calculate what you could give that would require adjusting your lifestyle. Give that amount. The sacrifice will focus your attention and deepen your trust.

Take reputational risks for your faith. Let people know you're Christian. Explain why you make decisions based on faith. Invite someone to church. Defend Christian positions when they're attacked. The risk of rejection or mockery will test whether your faith is genuine.

Pursue costly obedience. When you sense God calling you to do something difficult, do it. Volunteer for the ministry that scares you. Have the hard conversation. Make the apology that costs your pride. Forgive the person who doesn't deserve it. Choose obedience over comfort.

Serve people who can't repay you. Find ways to serve that offer no social benefit, no networking opportunity, no resume builder. Serve people society ignores: the poor, the imprisoned, the elderly, the disabled. The absence of benefit will clarify your motives.

Integrate faith and life. Stop compartmentalizing your Christianity. Let your faith inform your professional decisions, your financial choices, your entertainment, your relationships. When faith governs all of life, it naturally costs something in all of life.

Join a community with expectations. Find believers who will challenge you, hold you accountable, and expect you to grow. Avoid communities where everyone maintains appearances and nobody asks hard questions. Real community requires vulnerability, which is costly but formative.

Examine what you're unwilling to sacrifice. Make a list of things you're not willing to give up for Christ. That list reveals your actual priorities. Consider whether Christ should rank below those things. If he shouldn't, start subordinating them to him.

The Witness of Skin in the Game

Christians with skin in the game provide powerful witness. Their lives demonstrate that they believe Christianity is true in ways that words alone never can. When someone sacrifices career advancement for ethical reasons, observers notice. When someone gives away significant wealth, people ask why. When someone serves people nobody else serves, it raises questions. This witness is more persuasive than arguments because it's existential rather than intellectual. Anyone can argue for Christianity. Arguments are cheap. But when someone stakes their life on Christianity being true, it suggests they've found something worth staking their life on. That authenticity attracts attention in ways theoretical Christianity never does. Paul writes, "*Let your manner of life be worthy of the gospel of Christ*" (Philippians 1:27). A worthy manner of life means living as if Christianity is true, staking real things on it being true, accepting costs that only make sense if it's true. That kind of life witnesses to the reality of faith in ways that safe, comfortable Christianity cannot.

The Path Forward

Faith with skin in the game transforms believers. When Christians stake something real on Christ being true, their conviction deepens, their witness gains credibility, and their growth accelerates. Cost clarifies. Risk refines. Sacrifice proves what mere agreement cannot. This witness matters especially for the next generation. Young people watch their parents to see if Christianity is real or performative. If parents talk about faith but never sacrifice for it, the message is clear: this isn't something worth staking a life on. If parents make costly decisions because of their faith, children learn that Christianity matters enough to cost something. Yet parents who understand this principle for themselves often abandon it when raising children. They invest their own reputation, resources, and comfort in following Christ, then work to ensure their kids never face similar costs. They want their children to have faith without the difficulties that formed their own.

The instinct is understandable. Parents love their children and want to protect them. But protection from all spiritual challenge produces the very fragility examined throughout this book. Children whose faith is never tested develop faith that cannot withstand testing. Kids who never struggle with hard questions collapse when questions finally come. Young people shielded from every failure never learn to recover from failure. The same principles that build antifragile faith in adults apply to children, adjusted for age and capacity. The question is how to expose them to beneficial stress without overwhelming them, how to let them struggle without abandoning them, and how to prepare them for a hostile world without either hiding them from it or throwing them into it unprepared.

Chapter Six

Raising Antifragile Children

Karen's twelve-year-old daughter Emma came home from school confused. Her science teacher had explained evolution, and Emma wondered how it fit with the Genesis account she'd learned at church. Karen panicked internally. This was the kind of question she'd hoped to avoid until Emma was older, maybe in college when her faith was stronger. Karen redirected quickly. "That's a complicated topic, sweetie. What's important is that God created everything. Your teacher must teach what's in the textbook, but we know the truth from the Bible." Emma nodded and went to her room. Karen felt relieved. Crisis averted.

Meanwhile, Karen's friend Beth had a similar conversation with her thirteen-year-old son Todd. When Todd asked about evolution, Beth said, "That's a great question. Let me think about how to explain this well." That evening, Beth pulled out her laptop. She and Todd watched a video from a Christian biologist explaining different views Christians hold on creation. They discussed questions Todd had. Beth admitted she didn't have all the answers but showed Todd resources for thinking through the issues. They agreed to keep talking about it. Five years later, Emma's faith collapsed in her first semester of college. A biology professor presented evolutionary theory with compelling evidence. Emma remembered her mom dismissing the topic. She realized she'd been shielded from serious engagement with science. She felt deceived and unprepared. Within months, she decided Christianity was incompatible with intellectual honesty.

Todd faced similar challenges in college, but he'd already wrestled with these questions. He knew Christians held different views. He'd read arguments on multiple sides. When his professor presented evolution, Todd engaged thoughtfully rather than defensively. He asked good questions. He wasn't threatened because his faith wasn't built on avoiding hard questions. It was built on working through them. The difference between Emma and Todd illustrates the difference between fragile and antifragile faith formation. Karen tried to protect Emma from intellectual challenge. Beth exposed Todd to challenge in guided, age-appropriate ways. Karen's approach produced faith that couldn't withstand pressure. Beth's approach produced faith that grew stronger through engagement.

The Overprotection Problem

Modern parenting emphasizes protection. Parents protect children from physical danger with car seats, helmets, and constant supervision. They shield them from emotional harm with participation trophies and grade inflation. They guard against disappointment by intervening with teachers and coaches. They prevent boredom with scheduled activities. They minimize risk with rules and restrictions.

This protection seems loving. Parents want their children safe and happy. They want to spare them pain they experienced themselves. Many believe good parenting means minimizing harm and maximizing comfort. But overprotection produces fragility. Consider physical development. Children who never climb trees, never take physical risks, and never experience minor injuries develop poor balance, weak risk assessment, and fear of physical activity. Their bodies don't learn to handle stress. When they do fall or get hurt, they lack experience managing pain and recovery. The protection that seemed to keep them safe actually made them more vulnerable.

The same pattern appears in emotional and spiritual development. Children who never experience disappointment don't learn resilience. Children who never face consequences don't develop responsibility. Children who never encounter doubt don't build robust faith. The protection prevents the small stresses that would teach them to handle large stresses. Jonathan Haidt and Greg Lukianoff document this pattern in *The Coddling of the American Mind*. They show that the generation raised with maximum protection has higher rates of anxiety, depression, and fragility than previous generations. The very protections meant to keep them safe made them weak.

This applies directly to faith formation. Parents who shield children from questions produce children whose faith can't withstand questions. Parents who protect children from failure produce children who collapse when they fail. Parents who prevent children from experiencing consequences produce children who make reckless decisions because they've never learned that actions have costs. Antifragile parenting does the opposite. It exposes children to age-appropriate challenges in contexts where parents can guide them through the experience. It allows controlled failure that teaches without destroying. It creates opportunities for children to develop strength through difficulty rather than weakness through protection.

Exposing Children to Questions

Curt grew up in a church that discouraged questions. When he asked why God allowed suffering, adults told him not to question God. When he wondered about contradictions between science and Scripture, he was told science was wrong. When he raised concerns about things in the Bible he didn't understand, he was reminded to have faith. The message was clear: good Christians don't ask hard questions. Curt stopped asking questions out loud, but he didn't stop having them. The questions accumulated. By college, the weight of unanswered questions crushed his faith. He realized he'd been taught what to believe but not how to think about his beliefs. When professors raised objections to Christianity, Curt had no framework for responding. His faith collapsed. Contrast this with how Jesus engaged questions. People constantly asked him hard questions, some sincere and some designed to trap him. Jesus answered them. He used questions to teach. He asked questions that made people think deeply. He never dismissed questions as inappropriate or dangerous. He treated questioning as part of learning.

When Thomas doubted the resurrection, Jesus didn't rebuke him for lack of faith. He showed Thomas his hands and side, inviting him to verify the evidence (John 20:24-29). When John the Baptist sent disciples to ask if Jesus was really the Messiah, Jesus didn't chastise John for doubting. He pointed to evidence and let John draw conclusions (Matthew 11:2-6). Jesus took questions seriously because questions can lead to deeper understanding. Parents should do the same. When children ask hard questions about faith, parents can engage rather than deflect. This doesn't require perfect answers. It means taking questions seriously, thinking through them together, and showing children that Christianity can withstand intellectual scrutiny.

Carol's nine-year-old son asked why God didn't stop bad things from happening. Carol could have given a quick answer about the Fall or free will. Instead, she said, "That's one of the hardest questions people ask. Let's think about it together." They discussed what a world without free will would look like. They talked about how God uses suffering for growth. They acknowledged that some suffering seems pointless and no one fully understands it.

Allowing Failure and Consequences

Manual's parents constantly rescued him from consequences. When he forgot his homework, his mom brought it to school. When he quit activities after a few weeks, his parents found new activities rather than requiring him to finish commitments. When he spent all his allowance immediately, they advanced next week's allowance. By age sixteen, Manual had learned that his choices didn't really matter because someone would always fix the problems. Then Manual went to college. No one rescued him. When he skipped classes, he failed them. When he spent his meal plan money early in the semester, he went hungry. When he quit his part-time job after two weeks, he had no income. Manual was shocked. He had no experience managing consequences because his parents had shielded him from them his entire childhood.

Lelsie's parents took a different approach. When Lelsie forgot her homework in third grade, they let her receive a zero. When she didn't study for tests, she got bad grades and had to explain them at parent-teacher conferences. When she wanted to quit piano after six months, her parents required her to finish the year commitment before quitting. When she spent her allowance on impulse purchases, she had no money for the things she wanted later. Lelsie learned that her choices mattered. Bad choices produced bad consequences. Good choices produced good outcomes. She developed responsibility because her parents allowed her to experience the natural results of her decisions. By college, Lelsie knew how to manage her life because she'd been managing consequences in age-appropriate ways since elementary school.

This principle applies to spiritual life. Children need to experience the consequences of spiritual choices. This principle applies to spiritual life. Children need to experience the consequences of spiritual choices. When a teenager refuses to engage during family devotions—sitting silently, not opening their Bible, clearly disinterested—let them experience the spiritual emptiness rather than forcing enthusiasm you can't create. Continue the practice, maintain the expectation of presence, but don't manufacture their participation. When a child refuses to memorize the verse for Sunday school despite having time, let them experience the embarrassment of being unprepared rather than doing the work for them the night before. When a teenager won't serve with the family at the food bank, require their presence but let them sit bored rather than forcing cheerful participation—they'll learn either that service matters enough to engage or that disengagement has its own costs.

This doesn't mean abandoning children. It means letting them experience consequences while providing support and guidance. When Lelsie got a zero on her homework, her parents didn't lecture. They asked what she learned from the experience and how she'd handle it differently next time. The same approach works with faith. When consequences follow spiritual choices, parents can discuss what happened and why without rescuing children from the experience. The consequences teach what lectures cannot. Children learn that their relationship with God matters because they experience emptiness without it, not because their parents said they should value it.

Age-Appropriate Challenges

The key to antifragile parenting is matching challenge to capacity. Too much challenge overwhelms and destroys. Too little challenge produces no growth. The goal is appropriate stress that forces development without breaking the child. Physical trainers understand this. You don't put a novice under an Olympic weight bar. You start with weights they can handle and gradually increase the load. Each increase stresses their system appropriately, producing growth. The same principle applies to emotional and spiritual development.

For young children, appropriate challenges might include minor disappointments, small responsibilities, and simple questions about faith. A five-year-old doesn't need to wrestle with theodicy, but they can handle hearing that not everyone believes in Jesus and thinking about why their family does. They don't need adult responsibilities, but they can handle simple chores with real consequences for not completing them. For middle schoolers, challenges increase. They can engage with tougher questions about Scripture and theology. They can handle more significant responsibilities with more significant consequences. They can experience harder disappointments and work through them with parental guidance. They can start developing their own, possibly stronger, faith rather than simply inheriting their parents' faith.

For teenagers, challenges approach adult levels. They should be wrestling with serious intellectual objections to Christianity. They should be making moral decisions with real stakes. They should be experiencing the consequences of sin and repentance in their own lives. They should be practicing spiritual disciplines independently rather than only when parents enforce them. The progression builds capacity gradually. Each stage prepares for the next. Young children who learn that minor disappointments are survivable develop capacity to handle major disappointments as teenagers. Middle schoolers who practice making small decisions with consequences develop capacity to make large decisions wisely as young adults. Parents who skip this progression by overprotecting produce young adults who reach eighteen with the emotional and spiritual capacity of children. They've never developed strength because they've never faced resistance. When adult challenges hit them in college or career, they collapse because they lack the capacity that should have been building throughout childhood.

Modeling Rather Than Sheltering

Randy wanted his children to have strong faith, so he carefully controlled their environment. He monitored everything they watched, read, and listened to. He limited their friendships to children from church. He pulled them from public school to homeschool specifically to keep them from secular influences. He believed if he could create a pure Christian environment, his children would develop pure Christian faith. By high school, Randy's children knew theology but had never had to defend it. They knew Christian answers but had never encountered real objections. They knew they were supposed to believe certain things but had never chosen those beliefs in the face of alternatives. Their faith was theoretical, built in a greenhouse that bore no resemblance to the world they would soon enter.

When Randy's oldest son went to college, the son encountered viewpoints he'd never heard before. Evolution made sense to him. Relativism seemed reasonable. Christianity suddenly appeared narrow and antiquated. Within a year, he had abandoned his faith entirely. Randy was devastated. He'd done everything to protect his son's faith, and it had failed anyway. Meanwhile, Randy's friend Timi raised her children differently. She didn't shelter them from the world. She took them with her to serve in homeless shelters where they met people with different beliefs. She let them watch movies that portrayed perspectives different from Christianity, then discussed those perspectives together. She encouraged friendships with non-Christians. When her children encountered ideas contrary to Christianity, Timi engaged those ideas seriously rather than dismissing them.

Timi's approach was riskier. Her children heard objections to Christianity throughout their childhood. They met atheists, Muslims, and people of other faiths who seemed sincere and thoughtful. They watched their secular friends thrive in many ways. But Timi modeled how to think Christianly about all of it. She showed them how to love people who believed differently. She demonstrated that Christianity could engage with other worldviews without fear. Timi's children went to college with realistic expectations. They'd already encountered most of the challenges they would face. More importantly, they'd watched their mom handle those challenges with grace, wisdom, and confidence. Her faith wasn't fragile or defensive. It was strong enough to engage honestly with hard questions and different perspectives. Her children inherited that strength because they'd seen it modeled under real-world conditions.

The difference between Randy and Timi illustrates a key principle: children need models more than they need shelter. When parents model strong faith that engages the world, children develop strong faith. When parents create sheltered environments that avoid engagement, children develop greenhouse faith that wilts under real-world conditions. Jesus sent his disciples into the world (John 17:18). He prayed that God would protect them but didn't ask God to remove them from the world (John 17:15). He knew they needed to engage with the world while maintaining their faith. Parents should prepare children for the same reality: living faithfully in a world that doesn't share their beliefs.

Community Over Isolation

Farah's church had a robust youth program. Teenagers met weekly in small groups with adult leaders who knew them well. They discussed real struggles: doubt, temptation, peer pressure, family problems. The leaders shared their own struggles honestly. The community created space for teenagers to be honest about their faith journeys without pretense. Farah's daughter Ava participated throughout high school. She watched older students work through hard seasons and emerge stronger. She saw adults who loved Jesus but admitted their ongoing struggles with sin. She learned that Christianity wasn't about being perfect but about continuing to pursue Christ despite failure. When Ava faced her own crisis of faith at sixteen, she had community to support her. She texted her small group leader late one night, admitting she wasn't sure she believed anymore. The leader didn't panic or lecture. She met Ava for coffee and listened. Over months, Ava worked through her doubts with support from adults who took her questions seriously and peers who were asking similar questions. Ava's faith survived partly because she had community that made faith antifragile. She wasn't isolated in her struggle. She saw others struggle and work through it. She had adults who modeled honest faith. She had peers who encouraged her. The community created conditions where doubt could be expressed and addressed rather than hidden and festering.

Contrast this with teenagers raised in isolation from Christian community. Parents take responsibility for their children's faith formation without involving other believers. Children interact with adults at church but don't develop real relationships with them. Teenagers have no peer community working through similar challenges. When these isolated teenagers face doubt or struggle, they have no one to turn to. They can't tell parents because parents will panic or be disappointed. They have no trusted adults who aren't their parents. They have no peers who understand. The isolation makes faith fragile because there's no support system when pressure comes. The New Testament emphasizes community for good reason. Faith isn't meant to be individual. Christians need "one another" to confess to, encourage, challenge, and support. Children need community as much as adults do. They need to see that Christianity works in lives beyond their parents.

They need relationships with adults who can speak into their lives with perspectives different from their parents. They need peers who share their struggles and encourage their growth. Parents who try to be sufficient for their children's faith formation take on an impossible burden. You can't be everything your child needs spiritually. But you can connect them to community that provides what you cannot. That community becomes part of what makes their faith antifragile.

Teaching Them to Fall

Athletes practice falling. Martial artists learn to roll when thrown. Gymnasts practice landing safely. Skiers learn to fall without injury. The practice isn't intended to encourage falling. It's preparation for the inevitable falls that will happen. When athletes know how to fall, they can take greater risks because they know how to minimize damage when things go wrong. Spiritual parenting should include teaching children how to fall spiritually. Not because we want them to fail, but because they will. Every person sins. Every Christian struggles. Every believer faces seasons of doubt or distance from God. If children aren't prepared for these experiences, they can be catastrophic. If children know how to handle spiritual failure, they can recover and grow from it. This means teaching repentance as a normal practice, not a crisis response. Children should learn to confess sin daily, to themselves and to God. They should practice acknowledging when they're wrong and making amends. They should understand that failure doesn't end their relationship with God. It's an opportunity for repentance and growth.

It also means teaching children what to do when faith feels dry. Every Christian experiences times when prayer feels pointless, Scripture seems boring, and God feels distant. If children think this means they're not really Christians or God has abandoned them, these seasons can destroy their faith. If they understand spiritual dryness is normal and temporary, they can persist through it. Parents can prepare children for spiritual falls by sharing their own experiences honestly. When you struggle with sin, acknowledge it to your children in age-appropriate ways. When you go through times of feeling distant from God, let them know. When you fail and repent, model the process. Children who see their parents fall and recover learn that falling isn't the end. It's part of the journey. This requires humility from parents. Christian parents naturally want their children to see them as spiritual examples, which they are. But they are also fellow pilgrims who struggle and fail. Parents who pretend to have it all together teach their children that Christianity means maintaining appearances. Parents who are honest about their struggles while demonstrating how to handle them teach their children that Christianity means authentic pursuit of Christ despite failure.

The Long View

Modern parenting often optimizes for short-term peace over long-term development. It's easier to give in to a child's demands than to endure the tantrum. It's easier to rescue them from consequences than to watch them struggle. It's easier to answer questions with quick reassurance than to engage in difficult discussions. These choices produce immediate calm but long-term fragility. Antifragile parenting requires a long view. You make decisions based on what will serve your child at twenty-five, not what will make today easier. This often means choosing harder paths in the short term because they produce stronger outcomes long term.

When your child asks a hard question, the short-term easy response is dismissing it. The long-term strong response is engaging it, even though the conversation is more difficult and you might not have perfect answers. When your child fails, the short-term easy response is rescuing them. The long-term strong response is letting them face consequences and helping them learn from the experience. The long view also means accepting that you can't control outcomes. You can create conditions for faith to develop, but you can't force your children to believe. You can model Christianity, expose them to truth, provide community, and allow them to develop through challenge. But ultimately, each person must choose faith for themselves. Some children raised with every advantage abandon Christianity. Some children raised in terrible circumstances embrace it. This reality should humble parents without paralyzing them. Do what you can to create conditions for antifragile faith development, then trust God with outcomes you can't control. Your job is faithfulness in parenting, not guarantee of results.

Practical Steps

How do Christians practically raise children with antifragile faith? Several approaches help:

Answer questions seriously. When children ask hard questions about faith, engage them. If you don't know the answer, say so and research together. Show them that Christianity can handle intellectual scrutiny. Make it clear that questions are welcome and doubt is not the same as unbelief.

Gradually increase spiritual responsibility. Young children can pray before meals and memorize verses. Older children can lead family devotions occasionally. Teenagers can teach Sunday school, manage mission trip fundraising, and make their own decisions about spiritual disciplines and church involvement.

Be honest about your own struggles. Share age-appropriate information about your spiritual journey, including times you doubted, struggled with sin, or felt distant from God. Model how to handle these experiences without pretending they don't happen.

Connect them to Christian community. Provide opportunities for your children to build relationships with other believers, especially adults who aren't their parents and peers who share their faith. Youth groups, small groups, and mentoring relationships create support networks that make faith more resilient.

Expose them to different perspectives. Don't shelter children from ideas that contradict Christianity. Expose them to different worldviews in controlled ways where you can discuss together. Help them understand why people believe differently and how to think Christianly about alternative perspectives.

Practice spiritual disciplines as a family. Pray together, read Scripture together, serve together, and practice simplicity together. But also give children space to develop their own practices. By teenage years, they should be developing spiritual disciplines independent of your enforcement.

Celebrate repentance, not just obedience. When children sin and genuinely repent, celebrate the repentance. Make it clear that the goal isn't sinless perfection but authentic pursuit of Christ, which includes acknowledging and turning from sin.

Allow age-appropriate autonomy over faith. As children mature, give them more control over their faith practices. Let teenagers decide whether to attend youth group, how often to read Scripture, whether to go on mission trips. Give them ownership of their faith choices rather than forcing compliance.

The Goal

The goal of antifragile parenting isn't raising children who never struggle, doubt, or fail. It's raising children whose faith can withstand struggle, incorporate doubt productively, and recover from failure. This requires accepting that the path to strong faith runs through difficulty, not around it. Children need to encounter hard questions while they still have parents to help them work through answers. They need to fail while consequences remain manageable and guidance is available. They need challenges that stress their faith in contexts where support surrounds them. Parents who try to eliminate all challenge, answer every question before it's asked, and prevent all failure mean well. But they produce fragile faith that breaks under real-world pressure. Parents who expose children to age-appropriate challenge, engage questions honestly, and allow natural consequences produce antifragile faith that grows stronger through difficulty. The next generation will face a culture increasingly hostile to Christian belief. They'll need faith robust enough to withstand intellectual objections, costly enough to demonstrate genuine conviction, and antifragile enough to grow through opposition rather than collapse under it. That kind of faith develops through parenting that prepares children for difficulty rather than protecting them from it.

The Path Forward

But preparing children to engage a challenging world raises a question about the parents' own engagement. What kind of cultural posture are Christian parents modeling for their children? Some Christians respond to an increasingly secular culture by withdrawing entirely. They create parallel institutions, limit contact with non-believers, and focus on protecting their community from outside influence. Others take the opposite approach, engaging in culture war. They fight for political power, view secular neighbors as enemies to defeat, and measure success by legislative victories.

Neither approach produces antifragile faith. Withdrawal creates the very fragility this book has warned against, shielding believers from challenge rather than building capacity to meet it. Culture war ties faith to political outcomes, making it vulnerable to electoral loss and deaf to the people Christians are called to reach. A third way exists. Strategic engagement neither hides from culture nor fights it with worldly weapons. It enters the world as salt and light, maintains distinctive witness, and trusts that opposition can refine rather than destroy. This approach treats cultural hostility not as a threat to survive but as an environment where faith can grow stronger.

Chapter Seven

Engaging the Culture

In 2015, the Supreme Court legalized same-sex marriage nationwide. Christian communities responded in three distinct ways. First Baptist Church decided to withdraw. Their pastor preached a sermon series on being "in the world but not of the world." The church focused inward, emphasizing community among believers. They stopped hosting community events that might attract non-Christians. They started a classical Christian school where children could be educated apart from secular culture. The strategy was separation: build strong Christian community by minimizing contact with corrupting cultural influences. Crossroads Church declared culture war. Their pastor organized political rallies. The church became a hub for conservative activism. Sermons frequently addressed political issues and cultural decline. Members were encouraged to vote, protest, and fight against the moral decay they saw accelerating. The strategy was confrontation: reclaim culture through political power and public pressure.

Grace Community Church took a different approach. Their pastor acknowledged that many in the congregation disagreed about same-sex marriage and its legalization. He preached on how Christians should treat all people with respect and love while maintaining biblical convictions. The church continued hosting community events, including people with different beliefs. Members practiced hospitality toward LGBTQ neighbors without compromising their theology. They engaged conversations about sexuality with compassion and honesty. The strategy was engagement: live distinctly Christian lives while remaining connected to and in conversation with people who believed differently. Ten years later, the outcomes varied. First Baptist had grown more insular. Members knew Christian vocabulary and theology well but struggled to communicate with non-Christians. Their children felt prepared for Christian community but unprepared for secular universities and workplaces. The church was strong internally but had minimal impact beyond its walls.

Crossroads had become known for its political positions rather than its witness to Christ. Non-Christians associated the church with partisan politics. Some members had grown weary of constant cultural combat. Young adults often left, tired of angry rhetoric and political focus. The church had maintained its size but lost credibility beyond its base. Grace Community had become a place where people with questions felt welcome. Several members of the LGBTQ community attended, some becoming Christians, others simply exploring. The church had conversations that were sometimes uncomfortable but always respectful. Members learned to articulate their beliefs clearly while listening to people who disagreed. The church grew through relationships rather than programs or politics. These three responses represent the primary ways Christians engage culture: withdrawal, warfare, or witness through engagement. Each reflects different assumptions about how faith relates to surrounding culture and how Christians develop in relationship to cultural tension.

The Withdrawal Temptation

Throughout history, some Christians have responded to cultural hostility by withdrawing. The desert fathers fled Roman cities for Egyptian wilderness. Medieval monks separated into monasteries. Anabaptists formed insular communities. Each withdrawal aimed to preserve faith by limiting exposure to corrupting influences. The logic seems sound: the world threatens faith, so distance from the world protects faith. Create communities where Christian values dominate, where children learn biblical truth without secular interference, where believers can live according to God's standards without compromise. Build a parallel culture where faith remains pure.

Rod Dreher's "Benedict Option" articulates this approach for contemporary Christians. Dreher argues that Christians have lost the culture war and should focus on building resilient communities that can preserve faith through coming persecution. Rather than trying to change culture, Christians should create subcultures where they can live and raise children according to Christian principles. The approach has appeal. Cultural pressures on Christian belief are real and increasing. Children absorb secular assumptions through education, entertainment, and social media. Maintaining biblical convictions on sexuality, gender, religious truth, and moral authority requires swimming against cultural currents. Withdrawal offers relief from constant tension.

But withdrawal creates fragility. When you protect faith by limiting exposure to challenge, you produce faith that can't withstand challenge. The monastery might preserve orthodox belief, but it doesn't prepare believers to live faithfully in the world. When protected Christians eventually encounter secular culture, they often lack the capacity to engage it well. Consider the homeschool graduate who enters a secular university. If their entire education sheltered them from evolutionary theory, critical scholarship, or philosophical materialism, they're unprepared when professors present these views persuasively. They've been taught what to believe but not how to think about challenges to those beliefs. Their faith is fragile precisely because it was protected.

Or consider the church that focuses exclusively on internal community. Members know each other well and share common convictions. But they rarely interact with non-Christians. They struggle to communicate the gospel in language unbelievers understand. They have no relationships that might create opportunities for witness. Their faith may be strong internally, but it produces no external impact. Withdrawal also forfeits influence. When Christians separate from cultural institutions, those institutions become more secular by default. Education, media, business, and politics are shaped by the people who participate in them. Christian withdrawal ensures these domains are shaped entirely by non-Christian assumptions. Early Christians didn't withdraw despite facing worse conditions than contemporary Western Christians face. They lived in Roman cities, worked in pagan workplaces, and engaged with non-Christian neighbors. They maintained distinct practices and beliefs while remaining embedded in their culture. This engagement created tension, but the tension produced witness and strength rather than contamination and weakness.

The Culture War Temptation

If withdrawal is one extreme, warfare is the other. Rather than separating from culture, the culture war approach seeks to dominate it. The goal is reclaiming cultural ground Christians have lost: restore prayer in schools, reinstate traditional marriage laws, promote Christian values through legislation and political pressure. This approach sees culture as a battlefield where Christians must fight. The stakes are high: the soul of the nation, the safety of children, the preservation of religious freedom. Losing isn't acceptable, so Christians must organize, vote, protest, and pressure institutions to align with Christian values. The strategy is political power backed by mobilized believers. The culture war mentality produces several problems. First, it makes politics primary and gospel secondary. Churches become identified with political movements. Pastors spend more time on cultural commentary than biblical exposition. Members evaluate each other based on voting patterns rather than fruit of the Spirit. The church becomes a political bloc rather than a spiritual community.

Second, it produces enemies rather than mission fields. When you're at war, people on the other side are adversaries to defeat, not souls to reach. The culture war rhetoric treats non-Christians as threats rather than neighbors. This makes witness nearly impossible. People don't want to hear the gospel from people who view them as enemies. Third, it creates a self-righteous posture. Culture warriors often believe they're defending God and truth against darkness and deception. This conviction can produce arrogance and judgment. It's hard to maintain humility and compassion when you see yourself as fighting the forces of evil.

Fourth, it rarely works. Political victories prove temporary. Laws change. Court decisions get reversed. Public opinion shifts. Even when Christians win political battles, hearts don't change through legislation. Morality can't be imposed from outside. It develops from inside through the Spirit's work. Finally, it makes faith fragile by tying it to political outcomes. When Christians invest their identity and hope in political victories, political defeats threaten their faith. If we lose the election, if the court rules against us, if culture moves further from Christian values, despair follows. Faith built on political power collapses when that power fails.

Jesus explicitly rejected the culture war approach. When Peter tried to defend him with a sword, Jesus told him to put it away (John 18:11). Jesus's kingdom was not of this world, which meant it wouldn't advance through worldly power (John 18:36). His followers would conquer through sacrifice and service, not force and domination. Paul wrote that "*we do not wrestle against flesh and blood, but against the rulers, against the authorities, against the cosmic powers over this present darkness*" (Ephesians 6:12). The real battle is spiritual, not political. Fighting the wrong battle with wrong weapons produces wrong outcomes.

The Third Way: Strategic Engagement

Between withdrawal and warfare lies a third approach: strategic engagement. This means living as Christians in the culture without separating from it or trying to dominate it. It means maintaining distinct beliefs and practices while building genuine relationships with people who believe differently. It means speaking truth with compassion and listening to disagreement with respect. This approach sees cultural tension as opportunity rather than threat. When culture opposes Christian belief, that opposition clarifies what Christianity is. When believers face mockery or marginalization, they discover whether their faith is genuine or cultural. When following Christ costs something, nominal Christians are exposed while genuine Christians are strengthened.

Consider how the early church engaged Roman culture. Christians lived in cities, worked in typical occupations, and participated in community life. But they refused certain practices: they wouldn't worship the emperor, they wouldn't participate in immorality normalized in their culture, they wouldn't abandon infants, they wouldn't attend gladiatorial games. These refusals created tension. Christians were seen as antisocial, unpatriotic, and strange. They faced mockery, social ostracism, and eventually persecution. But their differentiation also created curiosity. Why would people risk so much for their beliefs? What did they know that produced such conviction and such different lives?

The Christian response to that curiosity was neither withdrawal nor warfare. They didn't retreat into isolated communities. They didn't try to overthrow Roman government. They lived among their neighbors, worked alongside them, and served them. When plague hit cities and pagans fled, Christians stayed to care for the sick. When disasters struck, Christians shared resources with neighbors. Their practical love made their verbal witness credible. This combination of differentiation and engagement proved powerful. Christians were obviously different, but their difference produced service rather than superiority. They held convictions firmly but expressed them winsomely. They maintained moral standards without judging those who didn't share them. The witness was both clear and attractive.

Daniel modeled this in Babylon. He served a pagan king faithfully while maintaining distinct religious practices. He interpreted dreams, advised on policy, and performed governmental duties with excellence. But he wouldn't eat the king's food, wouldn't worship idols, and wouldn't stop praying to God even when it meant facing lions. His excellence and his distinctiveness together created powerful witness. Strategic engagement requires confidence that Christianity is true and robust enough to withstand challenge. If you're secure in your faith, you don't need to attack those who disagree or hide from their arguments. You can engage respectfully, listen genuinely, and speak honestly. You can have friends who believe differently without compromising your convictions. It also requires humility. You might be wrong about some things. Your understanding of Scripture might be limited or distorted in places. Other people might have insights worth hearing even when you disagree with their conclusions. Engagement means being willing to learn even as you stand firm on core convictions.

Learning from Opposition

When Christians engage culture, opposition is inevitable. The gospel offends secular sensibilities. Christian sexual ethics contradict cultural norms. Claims about Jesus being the only way to God strike many as arrogant. These aren't bugs in Christianity, they're features. The offense is part of the message. The question is how believers respond to opposition. The fragile response is defensiveness: attack critics, dismiss objections, and retreat to safe spaces where everyone agrees. The antifragile response is learning: listen to criticism, examine objections honestly, and let opposition refine understanding and sharpen communication.

Geoff pastored a church in a progressive city. When he preached on biblical sexuality, a local newspaper published an opinion piece calling his views bigoted and harmful. Geoff's initial instinct was defensive. He wanted to write a rebuttal explaining why the columnist was wrong and unfair. But Geoff's mentor advised differently. "What if the criticism contains truth you need to hear? Maybe not about your theology, but about how you communicate it or how you treat people." Geoff read the column carefully. Some points were unfair, but others were valid. He realized his sermons on sexuality focused heavily on what Christians were against without adequately explaining what Christians were for: the goodness of God's design for human sexuality and relationship.

Geoff wrote a response, but not the one he originally intended. He acknowledged where the columnist's concerns were fair. He explained more fully the Christian vision for sexuality. He invited conversation. The exchange didn't convert anyone, but it opened dialogue. Several people from the LGBTQ community contacted Geoff to talk. Some eventually visited his church. The opposition had forced Geoff to clarify and improve his communication. This pattern repeats throughout history. Heresies forced the early church to articulate orthodox doctrine more precisely. The Reformation forced the Catholic Church to address corruption and clarify its teaching. Enlightenment criticism forced Christians to develop more sophisticated defenses of faith. Atheist objections have produced better Christian apologetics. Opposition consistently refines and strengthens Christian thought.

But this only works when Christians engage opposition rather than dismissing it. If you assume all criticism is bad faith or all objections are stupid, you learn nothing. If you take criticism seriously, even when it comes from hostile sources, you often discover ways to improve your understanding or communication. Paul engaged critics constantly. Jews objected that his gospel undermined the law. Paul didn't dismiss their concern. He addressed it directly in Romans, showing how the gospel fulfilled the law rather than abolishing it. Greek philosophers mocked the idea of resurrection. Paul didn't retreat from the doctrine. He articulated it more carefully and explained why it mattered. Opposition refined Paul's theology and communication.

The Witness of Differentiation

Christians become more compelling witnesses when their lives differ visibly from surrounding culture. The difference creates questions that create opportunities for gospel conversations. If Christians look identical to everyone else in priorities, practices, and problems, why would anyone be interested in Christianity? Consider several areas where Christian differentiation creates witness:

Marriage and sexuality. Cultural norms around marriage, sex, and gender have shifted dramatically. Christians who maintain lifelong, faithful marriages in a culture of divorce and serial relationships demonstrate something different. Christians who practice chastity before marriage and fidelity within marriage stand out. Christians who understand gender as created reality rather than personal choice differ from cultural consensus. These differences often produce criticism and mockery. But they also produce curiosity. Why do Christians make commitments others find unrealistic? What do they believe that enables those commitments? The difference creates opportunities to explain the Christian vision of human relationship and why it matters.

Generosity and simplicity. Cultural norms encourage accumulation, consumption, and financial security above all else. Christians who give generously, live simply, and prioritize relationships over possessions differ visibly. Their differentiation raises questions: Why aren't they focused on getting ahead? What matters more to them than wealth? How can they be so generous?

Grace and forgiveness. Culture encourages holding grudges, nursing grievances, and demanding justice. Christians who forgive enemies, reconcile relationships, and show grace to people who wronged them demonstrate something countercultural. Their actions prompt questions about where they find the capacity to forgive and why they believe forgiveness matters.

Community and hospitality. Increasing cultural fragmentation produces isolation and loneliness. Christians who build genuine community and practice hospitality toward outsiders offer something many people lack. Visitors to Christian communities often comment on the warmth and connection they observe. The community itself becomes witness.

Hope in suffering. Cultural responses to suffering typically involve either stoic endurance or angry complaint. Christians who maintain hope, find meaning, and even express joy in suffering look different. Their response to trials prompts questions about their source of hope and their understanding of suffering's purpose.

Each differentiation creates tension with cultural norms. The tension produces pressure on Christians. But the pressure is what makes the witness powerful. When Christians maintain distinct practices despite social cost, it suggests those practices stem from genuine conviction rather than cultural conformity. The cost validates the witness.

Cultural Engagement as Formation

Engaging culture doesn't just create witness opportunities, it develops faith. Christians who live faithfully in secular contexts develop capacities that Christians in protected environments don't need. Denise worked in a corporate environment where Christian belief was privately tolerated but publicly mocked. When she mentioned going to church, coworkers made jokes about imaginary sky beings and fairy tales. When moral conversations arose, her Christian perspective was dismissed as outdated or bigoted. The environment was hostile enough to create constant low-level pressure but not hostile enough to prevent her from functioning. The pressure forced Denise to think carefully about her faith. She couldn't just repeat phrases she'd heard at church. She had to understand why she believed what she believed and articulate it clearly. She had to respond to objections she'd never considered. She had to maintain convictions while surrounded by people who rejected them.

Ten years in that environment developed Denise in ways a decade in a Christian workplace wouldn't have. She understood objections to Christianity and how to address them. She could communicate the gospel in language unbelievers understood. She had practiced living faithfully when faith was costly. Her faith was strong precisely because it had been tested repeatedly. This is why cultural pressure produces antifragile Christians. It forces development that comfort doesn't require. Christians who never have to defend their faith or explain their practices don't develop those capacities. Christians who regularly face challenges develop skills and depth through the necessity of responding.

Paul seemed to understand this. He sent Timothy to difficult contexts rather than easy ones. He praised churches facing persecution more highly than comfortable churches. He described suffering as producing endurance, character, and hope (Romans 5:3-5). He saw opposition as formative, not just unfortunate. Modern Christians can choose to put themselves in environments that create this kind of formative pressure. Work in secular workplaces rather than only Christian organizations. Live in diverse neighborhoods rather than exclusively Christian communities. Build friendships with non-Christians rather than socializing only with believers. Read books by authors who challenge your views rather than only books that confirm them. These choices feel risky because they expose faith to challenge. But the exposure is what produces strength. Faith that's never tested remains untested. Faith that faces regular challenges and persists develops the kind of antifragile conviction that can't be shaken.

Practical Engagement

How do Christians engage culture strategically rather than withdrawing or warring? Several practices help:

Build genuine friendships with non-Christians. Don't see unbelievers as projects to convert or enemies to defeat. Get to know them as people. Listen to their stories. Understand their perspectives. Genuine friendship creates natural contexts for faith conversations that feel like sharing rather than preaching.

Participate in community institutions. Serve on school boards, volunteer at community organizations, attend neighborhood meetings, coach youth sports. Christian presence in these contexts influences them through participation. It also creates relationships that make witness possible.

Speak truth with compassion. When Christian perspectives differ from cultural norms, explain them clearly without attacking those who disagree. Focus on what Christians are for, not just what they're against. Show how Christian beliefs produce human flourishing, not just arbitrary restrictions.

Listen before speaking. When people object to Christianity or criticize Christian positions, listen carefully. Understand their concerns before responding. You might learn something. You'll communicate better after genuinely hearing their perspective.

Maintain differentiation without superiority. Live according to Christian convictions but without judging those who don't share them. Your distinct practices should reflect obedience to God, not superiority to neighbors. Let your life raise questions rather than proclaiming condemnation.

Serve regardless of response. Practice hospitality and service toward neighbors regardless of their beliefs or how they treat Christians. Love enemies as Jesus commanded. This kind of love subverts opposition and creates witness more powerful than arguments.

Form Christians for engagement. Churches should prepare members to live faithfully in secular contexts rather than only in Christian environments. Teach them to articulate faith clearly. Help them understand objections they'll face. Equip them to maintain convictions under pressure. Create community that supports engagement rather than requiring isolation.

Engage political issues without becoming partisan. Christians can and should care about justice, life, religious freedom, and moral issues. But our primary identity is Christian, not Republican or Democrat. Speak prophetically to both parties. Maintain independence from political movements. Make the gospel your primary message, not your political positions.

Expect opposition and learn from it. Don't be surprised when culture opposes Christian belief. Don't waste energy being offended or defensive. Instead, let opposition refine your understanding and sharpen your communication. See criticism as feedback that can improve your witness.

Focus on local faithfulness. You probably can't change national culture or win cultural wars. But you can be faithful in your workplace, neighborhood, and relationships. Focus on the people God has placed in your life rather than trying to influence people you'll never meet through political activism or online arguments.

The Long Obedience

Cultural engagement is a long-term project. You probably won't see dramatic results. Your neighbor might not convert. Your coworker might not appreciate your witness. Culture might continue moving away from Christian values. But faithfulness matters regardless of visible outcomes. Jeremiah prophesied to people who didn't listen for forty years. Noah preached while building the ark with no converts beyond his family. The prophets were largely ignored by the people they served. Success wasn't measured by results but by faithfulness to the call. Modern Christians often want quick returns. Success is measured by numbers: conversions, attendance, cultural influence. But biblical success is obedience. Did you love your neighbor? Did you speak truth? Did you live faithfully? Did you maintain hope? These are the measures that matter. Cultural engagement is also generational. The impact you have might not be visible in your lifetime. Children who watch you engage culture faithfully might be influenced decades later. Seeds you plant through relationships and service might not grow for years. The witness you bear might reach people you never meet through people you did reach. This requires confidence that God is sovereign over outcomes. You're responsible for faithfulness, not results. God handles the harvest. Your job is planting and watering (1 Corinthians 3:6-7). This understanding relieves pressure to win cultural battles or produce conversions. It focuses you on the daily work of living and speaking faithfully wherever God has placed you.

The Path Forward

Strategic engagement offers a path between withdrawal and culture war. It enters the world without adopting its methods, maintains distinctive witness without demanding cultural dominance, and trusts that opposition can refine faith rather than destroy it. This posture positions Christians to be salt and light in a culture that desperately needs both. But strategic engagement requires something modern Christianity often lacks: patience. The early church didn't transform the Roman Empire in a generation. Wilberforce fought slavery for forty-six years before seeing abolition. The underground church in China has been growing for decades, not months. Antifragile faith plays a longer game than our instant-gratification culture encourages. This principle extends beyond cultural engagement. Everything discussed in this book requires thinking in terms of years and decades rather than days and weeks. Spiritual disciplines build capacity through sustained practice. Quick repentance shapes character over time. Costly obedience forms us through repeated choices. Raising antifragile children unfolds across their entire development. None of this emerges from a weekend conference or a six-week program. The final piece of the antifragile framework is learning to take the long view: embracing sustainable practices over heroic efforts, measuring success across generations rather than news cycles, and trusting the slow work of God even when immediate results remain invisible. This long view ultimately rests on the deepest reality of Christian faith: the resurrection pattern that transforms death into life.

Chapter Eight

The Long View

Pastor Tony had been at City Church for two years when the board asked about his five-year strategic plan. They wanted metrics: attendance targets, budget projections, program launches. They wanted to know how many people would be attending in five years and what initiatives would get them there. Tony thought carefully before responding. "I can give you a five-year plan with numbers and programs. But I don't think that's what we need. Most churches grow quickly through programs and charisma, then collapse when the program ends or the leader leaves. I'd rather spend five years building something that lasts fifty." The board was skeptical. What would that look like?

Tony explained his vision. "We'll develop leaders slowly and carefully rather than recruiting volunteers quickly. We'll emphasize deep discipleship over broad programs. We'll build practices and culture that can survive my departure or difficult seasons. We'll measure success by how people's lives change over years, not how many people show up this Sunday. We'll think generationally rather than quarterly." The board agreed to try it, though some members had doubts. Five years later, the church hadn't grown dramatically. Attendance increased modestly from 250 to 320. But other changes were significant. Fifteen people who had gone through leadership development were teaching, mentoring, and serving effectively. Giving had increased not because of campaigns but because people had learned generosity through gradual practice. Small groups met consistently, with high retention and genuine community. Members could articulate their faith clearly and lived differently from their neighbors in visible ways. More importantly, the church had weathered two crises that would have destroyed less stable congregations. When Tony took a three-month sabbatical, the church continued strong under elder leadership. When a doctrinal controversy divided many churches in their network, City Church discussed it thoughtfully and remained unified. The foundation Tony had built proved solid.

Ten years later, Tony moved to another church. City Church didn't panic or collapse. The elders led the transition well. They called a new pastor who built on the existing foundation rather than starting over. The church continued growing slowly and steadily. Tony's long-term vision had created something that outlasted his tenure. This is the long view: building for sustainability rather than spectacular growth, developing people rather than running programs, creating practices that compound over generations rather than producing immediate results. It requires patience in a culture that demands quick returns. But it produces faith that thrives on disorder because it's built on foundations that can't be shaken.

The Personal Long View

Jason became a Christian at thirty. He was excited and threw himself into spiritual growth. He attended every Bible study, volunteered for multiple ministries, and tried to read through the Bible in ninety days. Six months in, he was exhausted and discouraged. His rapid-growth approach wasn't sustainable. He felt like he was failing spiritually. Jason's mentor suggested a different approach. "You're thinking in sprints. You need to think in marathons. What practices could you maintain for the next forty years?" Jason reflected and identified three: reading Scripture daily, praying regularly, and meeting with his mentor monthly. These practices didn't feel impressive. But his mentor assured him that consistency over decades would produce more growth than intensity over months.

Eight years later, Jason understood. The daily Scripture reading had given him deep biblical literacy. The consistent prayer had developed intimacy with God. The monthly mentoring had provided guidance through marriages, career changes, and spiritual struggles. The practices hadn't been spectacular, but they had been formative. Jason had built a spiritual life that could sustain him through whatever came. The personal long view involves several commitments:

Sustainable practices over heroic efforts. Choose spiritual disciplines you can maintain for years, not months. It's better to pray ten minutes daily for a decade than to pray two hours daily for two weeks. Consistency matters more than intensity. Small practices sustained over time produce more growth than dramatic practices that can't be maintained.

Process over outcomes. Focus on faithfulness rather than results. You can't control whether God uses your evangelism to convert someone. You can control whether you share your faith when opportunities arise. You can't control whether your prayers are answered the way you want. You can control whether you pray consistently. Measure yourself by obedience, not outcomes.

Formation over information. Knowledge matters, but character matters more. Don't just accumulate biblical information. Let Scripture form you into Christ's image. This takes time. You don't become patient by learning that patience is a virtue. You become patient through years of practicing patience in difficult circumstances. Character develops slowly through repeated practice.

Relationships over programs. Invest in a few deep relationships rather than many shallow ones. Find a mentor who can guide you over years. Build friendships with believers who will walk with you through seasons of struggle and growth. Join a community where people know you well enough to speak truth and offer genuine support. These relationships create stability that programs can't provide.

Long obedience in the same direction. Eugene Peterson's phrase captures the essence of discipleship. Spiritual maturity comes through consistent faithfulness over time, not through peak experiences or rapid transformation. Most growth happens gradually through daily choices to follow Christ in ordinary circumstances. Trust the process even when progress feels slow.

The personal long view requires patience with yourself. You'll fail repeatedly. You'll make the same mistakes multiple times. Growth will feel slower than you want. But if you maintain consistent practices and keep returning to Christ after failures, transformation happens. The person you are at forty will be dramatically different from the person you were at thirty, not because of one dramatic event but because of ten thousand small choices to follow Christ.

The Family Long View

Rachel and Chuck started having family devotions when their oldest child turned four. They read a Bible story, asked simple questions, and prayed together. The practice took ten minutes. Their children didn't always pay attention. They sometimes wondered if it mattered. Fifteen years later, they understood its value. Their oldest daughter was in college and facing challenges to her faith. But she had Scripture knowledge and prayer habits formed through years of family devotions. Their middle son struggled with anxiety and found comfort in Psalms he'd memorized during childhood family times. Their youngest daughter naturally turned to prayer when problems arose because it was her default, formed through years of family practice. The practice hadn't guaranteed outcomes. But it had laid foundation that proved valuable when tested. Chuck and Rachel hadn't seen results for years. They had simply been faithful, trusting that consistency would compound. The family long view involves:

Generational discipleship. Parents are raising not just their children but potentially their children's children. The faith you model and teach might influence grandchildren you haven't met yet. Practices you establish might become family traditions that last generations. Think about what you want your great-grandchildren to inherit spiritually and work backward from there.

Consistent practices over sporadic intensity. Family devotions five minutes daily teach more than occasional extended family worship times. Consistent mealtimes together build more connection than elaborate family events a few times per year. Regular service as a family forms character more than annual mission trips. Establish rhythms you can maintain through all seasons of family life.

Character formation over behavior management. Focus on developing virtues, not just controlling conduct. When your child lies, don't just punish the lie. Discuss why truthfulness matters and help them practice honesty. When they're selfish, talk about generosity and create opportunities to practice it. You're forming who they're becoming, not just managing who they are now.

Preparation over protection. We covered this in Chapter 6, but it bears repeating: prepare children for the world they'll enter rather than protecting them from it indefinitely. Expose them to challenges while they still have your guidance. Let them fail while consequences are manageable. Give them increasing responsibility as they mature. You're building capacity for adult faithfulness, not maintaining childhood innocence.

Multi-generational perspective. Your parents' faithfulness affects your children. Your faithfulness will affect your grandchildren. You're part of a chain. Sometimes you're planting trees whose shade you'll never enjoy, whose fruit your grandchildren will eat. That's not failure. It's faithfulness. Pray for generations you'll never meet and trust God to honor your investment beyond your lifetime.

The family long view requires resisting cultural pressure for immediate results. Your friends' children might appear more spiritually advanced at age ten. Your children might question faith when others seem certain. Your family practices might seem less impressive than others' elaborate approaches. But sustainable faithfulness over decades matters more than impressive performance in the moment. Trust the process. Keep doing the ordinary things faithfully. The compounding happens invisibly until it suddenly becomes visible in ways that surprise you.

The Church Long View

Valley Church was thirty years old when the founding pastor retired. The church had grown to 800 under his leadership. The search committee faced a choice: hire a dynamic young pastor who promised to grow the church to 2,000 or hire a seasoned pastor who emphasized depth and sustainability. They chose depth. The new pastor focused on leadership development, biblical literacy, and community. He didn't launch new programs. He simplified existing ones. He emphasized training over production. Growth slowed. Some members left for more exciting churches. But foundation was being built. Twenty years later, Valley Church had sent out three church plants that were themselves thriving. Dozens of members served in missions or ministry. The church had weathered pastoral transitions, financial difficulties, and cultural opposition without losing its identity or mission. Multiple generations attended, with young adults drawn by depth they couldn't find in trendier churches. The long-term investment had produced something sustainable. Other churches in the area had grown faster but collapsed when circumstances changed. Valley Church had built slowly and lasted. The church long view involves:

Leadership development over personality-driven growth. Invest in developing many leaders rather than depending on one gifted pastor. Create systems where leaders emerge from within rather than being imported from outside. Distribute authority so the church doesn't depend on any single person. This produces slower growth but greater stability. When leadership transitions happen, the church continues strong because leadership capacity is distributed.

Culture over programs. Programs come and go based on current needs and available volunteers. Culture persists across programs and seasons. Build a culture of discipleship, service, truth-telling, and grace. The culture will produce appropriate programs for each season rather than requiring you to maintain programs that may have outlived their usefulness. Culture also survives leadership transitions in ways programs don't.

Depth over breadth. It's more valuable to disciple twenty people deeply than to attract 200 people shallowly. The twenty who are genuinely formed will reproduce. They'll disciple others, plant churches, and influence their workplaces and neighborhoods. The 200 who attend services but remain unchanged will drift away when circumstances change. Measure success by transformation, not attendance.

Generational continuity. Churches should actively involve multiple generations. Young adults need the wisdom and stability of elders. Older adults need the energy and perspective of youth. Children need to see faith lived across ages. Single-generation churches lack depth and continuity. Multi-generational churches can pass faith and practice from one generation to the next naturally.

Patient planting. Church planting often focuses on rapid launch: gather a core team, start services, hit critical mass as fast as possible. An alternative is slow planting: spend a year or more gathering people, building relationships, establishing practices, and forming culture before launching public services. This takes longer but produces more stable plants. The foundation is solid before the structure is visible.

The church long view requires resisting metrics that measure only immediate results. Attendance, budget, and baptisms this year tell you something, but they don't tell you whether you're building sustainably. Better questions: Are people being formed into Christ's image? Are leaders emerging from within? Can the church survive the loss of key people? Will the church be stronger in ten years than it is today? These questions focus on sustainability rather than growth, depth rather than breadth, foundations rather than appearances.

Multi-Generational Thinking

William Wilberforce fought to abolish the slave trade in Britain for decades. He introduced his first bill in 1791. It failed. He introduced bills year after year. They all failed. Opposition was intense. Progress was imperceptible. Many thought his cause hopeless. Wilberforce persisted. He built coalitions, changed minds one person at a time, and refused to quit despite defeats. In 1807, Parliament finally abolished the British slave trade. In 1833, three days before Wilberforce died, Parliament passed the Slavery Abolition Act, ending slavery throughout the British Empire. Wilberforce's victory took forty-two years. He didn't live to see the full fruit of his labor. But his multi-generational perspective sustained him. He knew he might not see victory. He fought anyway because the cause was just and faithfulness mattered more than outcomes.

This is multi-generational thinking: working toward goals that might not be achieved in your lifetime, trusting that faithfulness compounds across generations. It requires:

Long-term vision beyond personal benefit. Work on things that will matter fifty years from now even if you won't be alive to see the results. Plant trees you'll never sit under. Build institutions that will outlast you. Invest in people who will carry on your work. Your legacy isn't what you accomplish but what continues after you're gone.

Patience with slow progress. Change happens gradually. You might spend a decade seeing little visible fruit. The temptation is to quit or change strategies constantly seeking faster results. Resist that temptation. Trust that faithful work compounds even when compounding is invisible. The seeds you plant today might not sprout for years. That doesn't mean they're not growing underground.

Focus on transmission, not just achievement. What you pass to the next generation matters more than what you accomplish in your generation. If you achieve great things but fail to develop people who continue the work, your achievement dies with you. If you achieve less but develop many people who carry on faithfully, your impact multiplies across generations.

Investing in formation systems. Create structures that form people over time: apprenticeships, mentoring relationships, discipleship programs, schools, and institutions. These structures outlive individuals and form multiple generations. The early church grew not primarily through evangelistic campaigns but through catechesis that formed converts over years. That formation created Christians who could withstand persecution and reproduce the faith.

Stories that carry vision across time. Tell stories of faithful people who worked toward goals they never achieved. Tell stories of small faithfulness that produced large outcomes generations later. Tell stories of perseverance through defeat. These stories inspire others to take the long view and persist when progress is invisible. They create culture that values faithfulness over results.

Multi-generational thinking runs counter to modern instincts. Contemporary culture demands quick results, measurable progress, and personal success. Strategies are evaluated based on whether they work now, not whether they'll work across decades. Lifetime achievement gets more attention than generational impact. But the kingdom of God grows like a mustard seed (Matthew 13:31-32), starting small and expanding gradually. It works like yeast (Matthew 13:33), affecting everything but often invisibly. It requires patience and trust that God is working beyond what anyone can see.

Practical Steps: Personal Level

What does antifragile faith look like in daily practice for individuals? Several concrete steps help:

Establish core practices. Identify three to five spiritual practices you can maintain for decades: daily Scripture reading, regular prayer, weekly worship, consistent giving, and regular service. Don't add more than you can sustain. Build these practices into your routine until they become automatic. When life gets chaotic, these core practices keep you grounded.

Build in deliberate stress. Practice spiritual disciplines that create beneficial difficulty: fasting regularly, practicing solitude monthly, simplifying your life annually, confessing sin weekly. These controlled stressors develop capacity for handling uncontrolled stress. They teach dependence on God, self-control, and spiritual awareness.

Maintain accountability. Meet regularly with at least one person who knows you well enough to ask hard questions and speak truth into your life. Give them permission to challenge you, point out blind spots, and hold you to commitments. This external accountability prevents drift and self-deception.

Put skin in the game. Make choices that cost you something because of your faith: give sacrificially, serve people who can't repay you, speak truth when it's awkward, forgive when it's costly. Let your faith affect your finances, career, relationships, and daily decisions in visible ways. The cost validates and deepens commitment.

Learn from failure. When you sin or fail, acknowledge it quickly. Confess to God and others. Examine what happened and why. Adjust your approach. The cycle of failure, repentance, and learning builds antifragile faith. Avoid the pattern of failure, hiding, and repeating.

Engage rather than withdraw. Stay connected to people and contexts that challenge your faith. Work in secular environments, build friendships with non-Christians, read books that question your views. The exposure creates opportunities for witness and develops capacity to articulate and defend your faith.

Practical Steps: Family Level

For families seeking to build antifragile faith in the next generation:

Establish family rhythms. Create sustainable practices you can maintain through all seasons: family devotions, regular mealtimes together, weekly service, annual traditions. These rhythms create stability and form children through repetition across years.

Model honest faith. Let children see you struggle with doubt, confess sin, wrestle with hard questions, and depend on God through difficulty. Don't pretend you have it all together. Authentic faith modeled imperfectly teaches more than perfect faith performed artificially.

Expose children to challenge. Let them encounter questions about faith, experience age-appropriate consequences, face intellectual objections, and work through doubt with your guidance. Protection produces fragility. Guided exposure to difficulty produces antifragility.

Prioritize character over achievement. Care more about who your children are becoming than what they're accomplishing. Emphasize virtues like honesty, kindness, self-control, and faithfulness over grades, awards, and success. Character formation takes longer but lasts longer than achievement.

Build multi-generational connections. Create opportunities for your children to learn from their grandparents, interact with elderly church members, and understand faith as something passed down through generations. Let them see that following Christ is a lifetime commitment that spans generations.

Tell family stories. Share stories of faith from previous generations: how grandparents came to Christ, how parents were sustained through trials, how God provided in difficult times. These stories create identity and perspective that extend beyond individual experience.

Practical Steps: Church Level

For churches seeking to build antifragile communities:

Develop distributed leadership. Establish plural eldership, train leaders from within, and delegate decision-making authority. Avoid concentration of power in one person or small group. Distributed leadership creates resilience and sustainability.

Emphasize formation over programming. Focus resources on discipleship, leadership development, and spiritual formation rather than on programs and events. Programs serve formation, not the other way around. Be willing to end programs that aren't producing formation.

Practice via negativa. Regularly eliminate unnecessary complexity, programs that have outlived usefulness, and activities that prevent focus. Create space by subtraction rather than always adding. Simplicity creates clarity and sustainability.

Build for multiplication. When the church grows, plant new churches rather than building bigger. Send leaders and members to start new works. This distributes risk, develops more leaders, and creates networks that are more resilient than single large organizations.

Create transparent community. Foster culture where people can be honest about struggles without fear of judgment. Model confession from leadership. Celebrate repentance, not just victory. Transparency enables accountability and mutual support that make faith antifragile.

Take the long view on success. Measure health by depth of discipleship, strength of leadership pipeline, and capacity to weather storms rather than by attendance, budget, or growth rate. Build foundations that will support the church through multiple generations and pastoral transitions.

The Resurrection Pattern

All this builds toward one ultimate reality: the resurrection pattern of death leading to life. This is the deepest antifragility in Christianity. What appears to be ultimate defeat produces ultimate victory. What looks like the end is the beginning. The cross demonstrates this pattern perfectly. Jesus's death appeared to be catastrophic failure. The disciples scattered. The mission seemed finished. The enemies of Christ appeared to have won. But the apparent defeat was the victory. Through death, Christ conquered death. Through weakness, he displayed power. Through what looked like loss, he accomplished salvation. Paul understood this pattern: "*We were so utterly burdened beyond our strength that we despaired of life itself. Indeed, we felt that we had received the sentence of death. But that was to make us rely not on ourselves but on God who raises the dead*" (2 Corinthians 1:8-9). Paul's near-death experience drove him to depend on God in ways success never would. The suffering produced something the comfortable path couldn't.

He writes elsewhere: "*I want to know Christ and the power of his resurrection, and the fellowship of sharing in his sufferings, becoming like him in his death, that by any means possible I may attain to the resurrection from the dead*" (Philippians 3:10-11). The path to resurrection runs through death. You can't experience resurrection power without experiencing death in some form. This pattern appears throughout Scripture. Joseph was sold into slavery and imprisoned before becoming second-in-command of Egypt. Moses spent forty years in exile before leading Israel. David was hunted by Saul for years before becoming king. The prophets were rejected before being vindicated. Jesus died before rising. The apostles suffered before the gospel spread. The apparent defeats positioned people for greater victories.

The pattern continues in Christian experience. Marriages often grow strongest after surviving near-divorce. Faith deepens most after periods of doubt. Ministries gain credibility after failures they acknowledge and learn from. Communities bond most strongly after weathering crisis together. The death experience, the loss, the defeat becomes the pathway to resurrection life. This is antifragility at its deepest level. Not just gaining from disorder but gaining through death. Not just surviving stress but being transformed by it into something you couldn't become any other way. The pressure that threatens to break you is breaking away what doesn't belong, revealing and forming what God intends.

Living Toward Resurrection

Understanding the resurrection pattern changes how Christians approach difficulty. Trials aren't just obstacles to overcome. They're opportunities for death that creates space for resurrection. When suffering feels like it's killing something inside, it might be killing parts that need to die so resurrection life can emerge. This doesn't mean seeking suffering or romanticizing pain. Death is real, and it hurts. The cross was brutal. Jesus asked if the cup could pass from him. But he went to the cross trusting his Father. He embraced death because he trusted it would lead to resurrection. Believers are called to the same trust. When circumstances crucify plans, kill hopes, or bury dreams, the Christian trusts that resurrection follows death. The seed goes into the ground knowing it must die to produce fruit (John 12:24). Life is lost so it can be found (Matthew 16:25). Weakness is embraced because God's power is made perfect in weakness (2 Corinthians 12:9).

This perspective transforms everything. Career failures become opportunities for God to redirect you toward his purposes. Relationship losses create space for deeper connections. Financial pressures teach dependence you couldn't learn in prosperity. Health crises force you to face mortality and eternal realities. Each death experience positions you for resurrection you couldn't experience without the death. The resurrection pattern also gives hope for the church. Christianity in the West appears to be dying. Cultural influence is declining. Hostility is increasing. Numbers are dropping. This looks like defeat. But the resurrection pattern suggests it might be preparation for renewal. The "cultural" Christianity that's dying needed to die. What's being pruned might create space for resurrection of something more authentic, more faithful, more powerful. History supports this hope. The church has appeared to be dying many times: under Roman persecution, during barbarian invasions, through Islamic conquest, in the aftermath of the Enlightenment. Each time, death proved to be labor pains for new life. What emerged after apparent death was often stronger than what died.

The Practice of Hope

Living the resurrection pattern requires hope, specifically Christian hope. Not optimism that circumstances will improve, but confidence that God is working through all circumstances toward his good purposes. This hope doesn't deny reality. It sees death and suffering clearly. But it sees them in light of resurrection. Paul writes that we "*...rejoice in hope of the glory of God. Not only that, but we rejoice in our sufferings, knowing that suffering produces endurance, and endurance produces character, and character produces hope, and hope does not put us to shame...*" (Romans 5:2-5). Hope makes present suffering bearable because it sees future glory. Hope enables rejoicing in trials because it knows trials produce transformation. This hope is grounded in God's faithfulness demonstrated through Christ's resurrection. Because Jesus rose, Christians know resurrection is real. Because God raised Christ, they trust he will work resurrection in their circumstances. The historical resurrection of Jesus guarantees the pattern: death gives way to life, suffering produces glory, loss creates space for gain. Practicing this hope means:

Trusting God in darkness. When you can't see how good can come from your circumstances, trust that God sees what you can't. Job couldn't see God's purposes in his suffering. Joseph couldn't see how slavery and prison served God's plan. The disciples couldn't see past the cross to the resurrection. Sometimes you walk by faith when sight provides no comfort.

Looking for resurrection. When you experience death in some form, watch for resurrection. How is God using this loss? What's being formed through this suffering? Where do you see new life emerging? The resurrection doesn't always look like you expect. Joseph's resurrection was becoming a ruler, not returning to his family. But God was working resurrection even when Joseph couldn't see it.

Remembering God's faithfulness. Review how God has worked in your past. Times you thought you were finished but God provided a way forward. Losses that created space for gain. Deaths that led to resurrection. Past faithfulness builds confidence in future faithfulness.

Living hopefully before others. Your hope in suffering witnesses to resurrection reality. When you face trials with confidence that God is working, people notice. When you maintain joy despite circumstances, it raises questions. When you trust rather than despair, it demonstrates that your hope is built on something solid. This witness points others toward the resurrection hope that sustains you.

Conclusion: The Long Obedience

This book has explored how the concept of antifragility illuminates Christian faith and practice. We've seen that Christianity is meant to be antifragile: gaining strength from disorder, growing through opposition, and thriving under pressure. We've examined how this works historically, personally, relationally, structurally, and culturally. The application is both simple and demanding. Simple because the principles are clear: expose faith to challenge rather than protecting it, fail small and often rather than avoiding failure, subtract before adding, maintain skin in the game, build for generations rather than quick results, embrace the resurrection pattern of death leading to life. Demanding because these principles require patience, courage, and long-term thinking in a culture that demands quick results, maximum comfort, and personal success.

The question facing each reader is whether you'll build fragile or antifragile faith. Fragile faith seeks comfort, avoids challenge, requires protection, and breaks under pressure. It produces nominal Christians who abandon faith when following Christ becomes costly. Antifragile faith embraces challenge, learns from failure, engages culture, and grows stronger through difficulty. It produces disciples who persevere because their faith has been tested and proved true. The choice isn't one-time. It's made daily through practices you establish, failures you learn from, challenges you engage, and hopes you maintain. Each choice compounds. Small decisions to follow Christ in ordinary circumstances produce, over decades, transformation you can't imagine now. The person you'll be at seventy is being formed by choices you make at thirty, choices that feel insignificant now but compound over time.

Made in the USA
Coppell, TX
02 February 2026

70795229R00075